Stock Options Trading Strategies

The Best Step-by-Step Guide to Learn How to Trade Stocks and Discover How These TOP Traders Investment Strategies Will Help You to Create Your Financial Freedom

Jim Livermore

Table of Contents

Chapter 3: Trading With the Trend

Buying Calls

Market Awareness

Setting Profit Goals

Day Trading?

Trading Puts

Range Trading

Swing Trading

Chapter 4: Earning Money No Matter How the Stock Moves

The Two Strategies: Straddle and Strangle

When to use these Strategies

These Are Risk Limiting Strategies

Straddle

Calculating breakeven points

How pricing changes for straddles

When to Exit the Position

Strangle

Summary

Chapter 5: Introduction to Spreads

Risk of Assignment

These are Vertical Spreads

Introduction

Options trading is one of the most exciting ways to earn money from the stock market, and it's also one of the most accessible. Any trader can buy and sell options with only a few hundred dollars. However, options trading can be very tricky if you don't know what you are doing. You don't want to rush in and trade options without understanding how they work and what the strategies are.

In this book, we will explain what the options trading strategies are and why you will want to apply them. As you will see there are different strategies for different situations. What strategy you apply will in part depend on what you think the stock is going to do. Also, you will apply different strategies depending on what your goals are.

We will begin talking about the why of options trading strategies, and then we will investigate the most basic strategies that are used for generating income, covered calls, and protected puts. We will also discuss using LEAPS to generate income and make money from trading.

Then we will talk about the possibility of the stock making big moves, and how you can use straddles and strangles to earn money from these situations. We will also talk about when you should consider applying these strategies.

After this, we will talk about spreads. Our focus in this chapter will be on the bull and bear debit spreads.

Next, we will cover iron condors and iron butterflies. The iron condor is an interesting strategy used when a stock is ranging, and it is actually something that you sell on the marketplace.

Then we will wrap up the book with two chapters that will cover earning income using options. In the first chapter, we will talk about the risk mitigated strategy of selling credit spreads. Then we'll wrap up the book talking about selling naked, which supposedly means that you are selling lone puts and calls but without any backing. We will see that isn't entirely true, and show you how to avoid being assigned the stock.

Options trading offers many different opportunities, but you can't go into it with your eyes closed. We hope that this book will help you get into options trading and do it right by following the best strategy that meets your goals.

Chapter 1: Why Use Options Trading Strategies?

Let me begin by asking you a question. What is your goal when it comes to trading options? Many beginning options traders haven't even thought about this. If you answered "to make money," then you might be someone who is coming to the world of options trading without giving serious thought to why they are doing it. But you have to start there.

So the first thing you should do before jumping on board and starting to trade options is to figure out what your end goal is. Every trader should have a plan and stick to that plan, even when it seems like it is stalling. If you don't have a plan then you are just going to be haphazardly trading all over the place with no rhyme or reason. And even worse – you are going to be letting emotion get in the way of your trading.

Trust me, when it comes to options emotions get involved. Depending on what the market is doing, you might see your options melting right before your eyes. When that happens, emotions are going to come up in a big way and that can lead to bad decisions.

Of course, before that happens you need to mitigate your risks as much as possible. But it's not possible to account for everything, and sometimes things are just going to go south. The first thing you need to do is have a clear understanding of how options work. If you don't understand expiration dates, the Greeks, the differences between calls and puts, you need to go study those things right now. You need to know them before you jump off into different options strategies.

Speculating vs. Income

In my view, there are two basic ways that we can classify options trading. It's either speculating or income investing. Let's talk about speculating first. Basically, this is nothing more than guessing which way the stock is going to move and then buying options to profit from the guess. So if you think the stock is going to go up, then you buy a call. If you think the stock is going to go down, you buy a put option.

There are more complicated ways to do it, and there are some strategies too. We are going to be investigating some of them in this book. But you need to be clear about what you are doing if this is what you want to get into. A speculator basically hopes to trade with a trend in the stock market. Options can make money fast, but they can also lose money fast. Most professional options traders avoid playing the game using straight-up puts and calls. Doing that is probably the highest risk you can take while trading options.

That isn't to say that you can't win and win big just buying calls. Sometimes you can, and some traders are really good at it. But winning using that as a strategy takes a lot of time to study and frankly, most people aren't good enough at it in order to consistently make money.

Now let's turn our attention to the other possibility, which is using options in order to generate income. This is a more conservative way to get into the options world, but it has it's risks too. But if you play it right, you can sell options for income and build a pretty lucrative career.

So this is the first step. You need to decide if you are interested in trading options for speculation or for income. I've done both, but I would never recommend that other people do both and nowadays I stick strictly to the income side. But you have to do what you are most interested in. This is the first step to building an effective options trading plan.

Set Your Income Goals

The next step is to set your income goals. This is really to get you focused on a month to month basis, but you can also have a grand end goal in mind. I am sure that many readers of this book are hoping to ditch their day job and move on to trading options full-time. That is fine, but how much money do you need to make per year in order to get that done? Make sure that you've written this down and that you have a clear understanding of how much per month you need to make. Others might have a lofty number in mind, like becoming a millionaire.

You can become a millionaire trading options, but this is not something most people are able to do, and you are probably not going to be able to accomplish this overnight. If you want to become a millionaire in five years, you are going to have to make enough to live on, and then make $200k + on top of that. I put a plus there because guess what – if you are making that kind of bank then you are going to have to pay a lot of taxes too. This is something doable, but you are going to have to be very serious about it and be cautious about your trading.

Also, you can't start out thinking you are going to make something like $250k your first year. I encourage new traders to start out with reasonable goals that they can reach. Then each time you reach one of your goals, you set a new one and shoot for that.

So start small. You might start off with a goal of making a $500 profit your first month. You are going to be surprised but some people are going to find this very hard to do. But if you are able to do it, congrats – you can then make a new goal, like making $1,000 profit. Building up in this way you can eventually get where you want to be, and then reach your ultimate goal. What then? Options trading is fun, so most of you are probably going to be addicted to it and you will probably keep going. Don't get stupid about it and blow all your money if you manage to reach your goals. Keep playing conservative.

Learn the Strategies

Options trading is very risky. The reason is that options magnify small changes in stock price. I know many people are going to say, yeah but I can buy an option for a hundred bucks. If I lose it, what's the big deal?

There is some truth to that, but after you start trading regularly, you are probably going to be trading more than a single option. So this can get serious real fast, and some people, lots of people, have lost their shirts just trading options carelessly. You don't want to be one of those people, which is one of the reasons that you are reading this book.

To trade successfully, you should study all of the options trading strategies that are available, and then become an expert in one or two of them. Yeah, you heard me right. You don't want to be spreading yourself thin hoping to do and try everything. So you should pick the ones that are the most interesting do you and then move forward, with the hope of building a business out of it.

The next thing you should do is pick your five favorite stocks or ETFs that you want to trade. Just like strategies, you don't want to spread yourself too thin by trading any stock that strikes your fancy. Pick five to focus on at least for the next upcoming quarter, and better yet for a year. At the end of the period of time that you pick, you can evaluate the situation, and move one or more stocks out and replace them with different securities.

Why there are options strategies

To reiterate, there are options strategies because options trading is risky, and so smart people who study this stuff all the time have come up with ways to mitigate the risk. There are downsides to this. Let's look at a call option as an example.

With a call option, you have a limited risk unlimited reward financial asset. In practice, it's not really unlimited reward, but however much the stock might go up, you are going to make that much money x 100, roughly speaking. You might lose money, there is a good chance it could expire worthlessly. If that happens, you will be out $100 or whatever you paid for it. Of course, as I mentioned, when people really get into trading you are not going to be trading a single option. How else are you going to be making money? So if it expires worthless, you might be out $1,000, because you bought a lot of ten options.

So what options trading strategies do in most cases, is they trade away some of that upside to minimize risk. Using a trading strategy, you might have a higher probability of a win, and lower levels of risk, but in most cases, the amount that you can profit will be fixed. That might even sound boring to some people – but let me ask how boring that is compared to buying straight calls and losing $1,000?

Options Trading Levels

If you aren't aware of it, there are different options trading levels. So if you want to implement various strategies, you have to know what level you are, and how you get to a higher level. The lowest level, a level 1 trader, is pretty limited as far as what they can do. The most they can do is sell what is called a covered call. We will talk about what that is in the next chapter. A level 1 trader can also sell a protected put. Beyond that, they cannot trade options.

A level 2 trader is able to sell covered calls and protected puts, but they can also buy to open calls and puts. That means they can trade options back and forth, or as I called it at the beginning of this chapter, they can speculate. As I said, this can be profitable but it's pretty risky, and to be honest, for most people it's not going to be consistently profitable.

To do most of the strategies in this book, those outlined in chapters 4-7, you need to be a level 3 trader. In order to get this status, you will have to do an interview process with the broker. It's really not that complicated and most brokers are actually pretty lenient about letting people become level 3 traders.

In order to sell naked options, you have to be a level 4 trader. That is a little more difficult to obtain, and you have to open a margin account to do it. There are even a few brokers that don't allow people to do level 4 options trading, but that is kind of overkill if it's done carefully it's not really all that dangerous.

Margin Accounts

Since we mentioned it, we might as well tell you a little about it now. In order to sell "naked" options, which means they aren't backed by anything, you have to open a margin account. A margin account is just an account that lets you borrow from a broker. You must deposit a minimum of $2,000 in a margin account in order to open one.

The margin is the amount of cash in your account. You can then use leverage to trade 2x as much as you could using just your cash alone, so you basically borrow the rest from the broker. If you don't pay it back right away, then you will have to pay interest on it and repay the loan. The hope, of course, is that your trades don't go bad, and so you won't have to pay it back other than simply taking the money you won from the trade and paying a portion of that to the broker to close out the loan.

Of course, a smart trader isn't going to blow their entire account on a single trade.

Some other things you need to be aware of our buying power and margin calls. Even if you don't have a margin account, you are going to notice you have a certain level of buying power associated with your account, if you are doing things like selling credit spreads. Your buying power is just what it says it is, it's either the amount you have available to buy options, or it's the amount you have available to put up as collateral for specific kinds of trades.

A margin call is something that could happen if you lose more money on a trade than what the margin account can cover. A margin call is sometimes described as a demand from the broker to put more cash in your account. If you can't do it they are going to close all of your positions and send you a bill. So if you decide to open a margin account, you are going to have to use it carefully. Don't get yourself in a situation where a margin call might happen. If your trades are at risk, get out of them before you get into trouble. There is no sense of holding on using "hope" as a strategy. If a stock is declining, and it's ruining your options trade, don't sit there hoping that it's going to turn around. That is something that is not going to work and it's something that can wipe out a lot of new traders.

Don't get caught by time decay

Something that many new traders are aware of, and yet they continually ignore, is time decay. You need to be keenly aware of time decay. If you are buying options, time decay is your enemy, and it can be quite potent. As options get closer to their expiration dates, you are going to find that time decay becomes ever more important. So pay attention to it, and don't hold an option that isn't going well too long. If you do that, you can find yourself in a position where time decay eats you alive, and pretty soon you have a worthless option on your hands.

What's Next

Now that you have some basic knowledge under your belt, you should start setting up your options trading plan. Start with your goals and where you want to be a year from now. Also, make sure that you are recording every single options trade that you make inside a notebook. It's important to be completely honest with yourself about your trades. Don't just remember the wins and forget the losses. For the year, you want to have a running total that records either your profits or your losses. That is going to be a very important number to always have in mind so that you know where you stand and how far or close you are to your goals.

In the next chapter, we are going to start with level 1 trading, so we are going to learn about covered calls and protected puts. You can only do a covered call if you actually own 100 shares of the stock. So if you don't own stock, you aren't going to be able to make the trade. It's kind of ironic but the lowest level of trading is the one that has the highest bar to cross for many people.

Chapter 2: Covered Calls and Protected Puts

In this chapter, we are going to start by covering the simplest trading methods that there are, which are open to level 1 options traders. Basically, anyone is a level 1 options trader. To become a level 1 options trader, all you have to do is open a brokerage account. These are level 1 trading methods because they are low risk, in that the potential loss is completely accounted for by something that you own. In the case of a covered call that is going to be the stock that you already own. For a protected put, you have to put enough cash into your account in order to cover the potential losses.

Review: What is a call option?

Let's start by reminding ourselves what a call option is. A call option is a contract that gives the buyer the option to buy 100 shares of stock before the contract expires. The contract has the share price that the buyer would pay, should they choose to exercise the option. This price is called the strike price. In order for the option to be worth something, the market price of the stock has to be higher than the strike price. But more than that, there is a fee that the buyer has to pay to own the option. That fee is called the premium. So the option is not going to be worth exercising unless the market price goes above the strike price plus the premium that was paid to buy it.

Most people that buy call options have no interest in buying the stock, they just want to trade it back and forth, hoping to make a quick profit. These are the speculators, who are just hoping that the stock price will go up, making the option worth a lot more money. You can find out how much more by looking at the Greek quantity delta, which gives you the fraction that the price of the option will change by - per share – when the price of the stock goes up. But remember it also tells you how much it will go down too if that is what happens.

So if the share price goes up to $1, and the delta is 0.80, that means that the price of the option will go up to eighty cents per share or $80 in total. So the share price rise of $1 is magnified to $80 because the option controls 100 shares of stock. This is what makes options so appealing, but people forget that you can just as easily lose that $80 too.

The buyer of a call option is betting that the stock price is going to go up. Most of the time they are hoping to ride a trend, so they want to see the stock go up by a large amount. The trick is to get out of the option at the right moment when there are still people hoping that the stock is going to keep rising, even if it's starting to peter out. That may or may not happen, but it can happen.

Other times you might just be hoping to trade a ranging stock when it's going into its upswing. In that case, the possible profits on the stock might not be as great, but you are still able to earn some money. It can also be a quick in and out transaction, so you might find yourself making a day trade.

Now that we have reminded ourselves what call options are for, let's talk about selling one.

What is a covered call

In order to buy calls, someone has to originate the contract, or "sell to open." In this case, someone sells a call option, and they are agreeing to sell 100 shares of stock at the strike price if someone who bought the option decides to exercise the option. It doesn't matter how many times the option changes hands as it gets traded. Whoever owns the option can exercise it at any time, if the price moves in a way so that doing this would be profitable to them. So if you sell a call option, you might be in a position where you have to sell 100 shares of stock.

In the case of a covered call, you must on the shares of stock before you can sell the call. This is why a covered call is considered to be a low-risk trading strategy. A high-risk trading strategy using the example of a call would be selling the call but not having the stock in your possession or perhaps even having the money to be able to cover the deal. Although there are real risks that are involved, at least in the case of a covered call you already have the shares and so if someone exercises the option it won't be a problem going forward with the transaction.

So the first thing to consider is why would someone put their shares at risk in this way? The reason is that you can earn a regular income from the shares of stock that you own. The trick to doing it right is picking the best strike price so that there is a balance between the potential to make income and the risk of having to sell the shares. A big concept that you need to get into your mind if you're going to be selling covered calls is the break-even price. In fact, no matter what you're doing with options, the breakeven price is an important concept that always has to be looked at.

So let's summarize what a covered call is and how it works. We start with the assumption that you own at least 100 shares of some stock. Perhaps you own a lot more than this and you would be willing to risk several hundred shares or even thousands, in order to get the cash income. But for the sake of our discussion, we will just assume that you own 100 shares.

he way that this works it Is you can't just sell any old price that comes to mind and you can't make something up. You have to go on the market and see what call options are actually available for the stock that you own. We may as well take a specific example to get an idea of how this actually works.

For the example let us suppose that you own shares in the exchange traded fund QQQ by power shares. Looking up the options that are available in one months time we see that there are several strike prices in increments of $.50. So the way that you start out did you have to look up the options that are on the market and then pick up the strike price that you want to use in order to sell your option. The first thing you want to look at is the share price or market price that is the most recent one available. In our case, the share price is $186.95.

In the money, options sell for much higher prices as compared with out of the money options. However, selling and in in the money option is a risk. How much of a risk is going to depend on a couple of factors? The first factor is what the break-even price would be and the second factor is the volatility of the stock.

Can You Get Assigned?

The first thing you might ask is what is the real risk of assignment. For readers who aren't completely familiar with the jargon, assignment means that whoever bought the option is going to exercise their rights. In this case that would mean that they buy the shares from you.

Unfortunately, on the Internet, there is a lot of misinformation with regard to the possibility of assignment. You are frequently going to see the claim made that 85% or something like that of options expire without being exercised. Or sometimes you might read that 85% of options expire worthlessly. The details really don't matter, what we want to focus on is what might happen if you actually sell on an options contract. And what is frequently left out of this discussion is the question of whether or not the option is in the money or out of the money.

So let's cut to the chase. If you have an option that you have sold and it is in the money, when it expires, it is going to be exercised. So that means that you're going to have to sell your shares in the event that you let the option expire. So lesson number one for someone who wants to sell covered calls is that if they sell an option either in the money from the beginning, or it's in the money as the expiration date approaches, that means that you need to get out of this contract.

If you're planning to sell options, you should highlight the following statement. If you sell an option and it's in the money when the expiration date is approaching, you must buy back the option unless you are comfortable with it being exercised.

At first glance, it might strike you that's crazy to take an action like that. Some readers who are not very familiar with options might be saying to themselves that how are you going to make money? However, if that thought entered your mind, you are ignoring the friend you have as an option seller.

That friend is called time decay. You sell an option a month out, and what happens is the value is going to be decreasing as time goes on. Remember that an option has a value that comes from the underlying stock, but it also has a value from the time left until the options contract expires.

That means that more than likely the option is going to be cheaper by a large margin at the time that you buy it back then it was when you sold it in the first place. So we can sell options and then we can buy them back and we are going to make the maximum profit, but we might be making something like 85% of the possible profit that could be made. And even better we've made money while keeping our shares.

Don't forget that if the contract we are talking about is American style, which is going to be the vast majority of the contracts that you are involved in, the option could be exercised at any time between the date that it's issued, and the expiration date. However, although you can't predict with certainty what anyone buyer is going to do with it, statistics show it's unlikely to be exercised early. Don't let that give you too much comfort however, you have to be aware that it could happen at any time. That said, what we do know is it's unlikely and you also have the break-even price working in your favor, so what you really have to worry about is the situation where the option expired when it was in the money.

Let's take a look at a specific example to understand how this works. So we will go back to QQQ which is an exchange traded fund that tracks the NASDAQ 100. The share price is $186.95. Looking at the first in the money call the strike price is $186.50. That might seem a little bit close for comfort. But whether or not it really depends on the breakeven price and the volatility. For analysis focus on the breakeven price. It's $190.66. So how could that be? Well, that's because someone has to pay $4.16 in order to buy this option. So the fact that the option is a little bit expensive gives you a fair amount of breathing room before there would be any risk of assignment. But we could also look at selling out of the money options which is what most people do. So we could sell a $187.50 call option for $3.55. The breakeven price for that one is $191.05. So we gained about $.50 in breathing room. We could go even further out, one of the things that people look at when selling options is the chance of profit. Your broker should be giving you this information. Personally, I like to go with a chance of profit of 75%. So we can sell out of the money call option on QQQ with the strike price of $191. In that case, the breakeven price is $192.76. So it's more than $2 higher than the first one we looked at. That means it's far less likely to expire in the money.

If you are comfortably out of the money you can just go ahead and let the option expire. On the other hand, as we said with the strategy you can always buy it back a couple of days before the expiration date so that you don't have to worry about being assigned. But it's important to emphasize again that if you let an option that is in the money expire you will be assigned. The broker in most cases is actually going to go ahead and do the exercising of the option.

Let's look at how the strategy would work. Now let's imagine that the underlying stock price is $188 a share. If we had a strike price of $186, would 30 days left to expiration the option would be worth $538. Now let's consider 20 days left to expiration. At the point, the call has dropped in price to $460 if we keep every other characteristic constant. Now let's consider 10 days to expiration. At this point, the call has dropped to $361 in value. So by now, you should be figuring out that the time value which is lost every day is working strongly in favor of the seller of the call option.

But let's carry it all the way to two days before expiration. We are still imagining that the option is in the money by $2. Now the call is priced at $238. So if we had sold the option would 30 days left to expiration, we would have sold it for $538. So with two days left to expiration, we can buy it back for $238, and we've made a $300 profit. And by purchasing the option back, we have avoided the problem that would arise by letting it expire and then we would probably be assigned and have to sell the shares.

That is how the strategy works. So yes, we didn't make the entire $538 that we could've made had the option expired worthless. However, we still made a substantial profit. So let example was one that considered an option that was actually in the money. But what you should be doing is selling options that are out of the money so that you substantially reduce the risk of being assigned.

Income Strategy

The main strategy involves here is to utilize the shares of stock that you own in order to make some monthly income. If you own 10,000 shares, you could use 5000 of those shares and sell 50 options contracts every month. So if we made $300 from every contract, that would be a $15,000 a month income. But maybe we are getting a little bit ahead of ourselves because you might not own that many shares. Let's say you only own 500 shares. You can still earn $1500 if you sold five options contracts on those shares. That's a pretty good passive income and five options contracts is a lot easier to manage than 50.

The main goal that is used in this strategy is to be able to do this month after month. So you want to have that practice of avoiding being assigned either by showing out of the money for buying the option back so that you can keep your shares and repeat the process the following month.

Selling the Shares

That said, you should also be prepared for the possibility of having to sell the shares. So one thing that might be considered is you should work out a price that you would find acceptable as far as selling the shares and facing the prospect of losing them. It's fair to assume that you would not be doing this if you had paid a higher price for the shares than what you are using for your strike price. Of course, it would be a possibility but in most cases, people are going to be selling call options against shares that they had purchased in the past. So it won't be too painful in that kind of situation to go ahead and let your shares go.

In this case, we can look at the worst-case scenario. That would be you sell the shares but you get paid cash so you are not exactly in a losing situation. Not only do you get the cash from selling the shares, but if the option is exercised you also get to keep the entire premium paid. Just to get an idea of how this would work let's go back to our previous example. We have set up a call option with the strike price of $186. In our fictitious scenario, the share price on the market was $188. However, nobody would buy it at that price. Don't forget that the buyer of the option paid $5.38

per share. So they wouldn't exercise the option unless the price went to $191.38. And even then, do you think they would actually buy the shares using the options contract? The answer to that question is probably not. In order to be worth it, the share price actually has to move above the breakeven price. Once it does that, how much it has to go above the breakeven price is something that is subjective. It might be worth it to someone to buy the shares and make it $.50 cent profit per share. Somebody else, might not find that worth bothering with and instead of doing that they might try selling the option to somebody else. The reason that may be possible is that the price of the option might have increased.

And in fact, if we go to 10 days before expiration setting the share price to $192, the call option would be priced at $658. So in that situation, you are not going to buy it back. However, since most options traders are simply looking to profit by buying and selling the contracts rather than exercising the option they would probably sell it for $658 and take the profit that they made. This leaves you protected because whoever bought it for $658 is now facing their own breakeven price. The share price has to rise past the strike price plus the break-even price in order to make it worth it. So as you can see from this example it still wouldn't be worth exercising even though the option is in the money.

Now if the option was very deep in the money it might be worth exercising had the buyer purchased it hi there when it was barely in the money or if they were really lucky it was out of the money at the time.

Summary: Covered Calls

So the bottom line with covered calls is that if you wisely choose the strike price used, it's a pretty good strategy that can be used in order to earn some money off of the shares of stock that you already own. Unless you recklessly choose a strike price, the reality is in most situations that you are going to face you are not going to get an assigned and you will be able to keep your shares and play the same game the following month. Even in the event that you have to sell the shares, you would be lucky enough to get cash for the shares that you sold as well as pocketing the premium that you were paid for the option. So this is not a totally losing situation and you would be able to use the money to buy shares of stock in another company and then go back to using the same strategy. Level one traders are able to sell covered calls in the event that they own the shares of stock. So just to be clear, if you don't own shares of stock you are not able to sell covered calls. But as we will see later, you will be able to sell calls anyway.

Protected Puts

Now let's turn our attention to the other possibility that can be used by level, one trader. This is called a protected put. You can think of this as the opposite situation to a covered call. Well, actually it's not really the opposite situation so we might just say it's an analog in the case of puts. Just as we did in the previous example let's quickly review what a put option is all about for readers who are not completely clear about this notion.

A put option is equivalent to shorting the stock. So if you buy a put option, you are betting that the price of the stock is going to drop. Put options have the same characteristics otherwise than call options do. So they have a strike price which sets the boundary as to whether or not the option is worth anything. In this case, you want the market price of the stock to drop below the strike price. That has implications for the breakeven price. The same laws about money that we discussed in relation to the breakeven price for the call options apply here. However, the difference is you subtract the breakeven price from the strike price to get the first price at which there would be any risk of assignment.

So let's turn our attention to what happens if the option is exercised in this case. In case you don't remember if you are the buyer of the put option you have the option of selling 100 shares of the stock to the other party of the contract. Turning things around that means that if you sell to open a put option, in this case, you would have to buy 100 shares of stock at the strike price. Let's say that the stock was trading at $140 a share. To buy 100 shares you would need to cough up $14,000.

So what does it mean to say that a put is protected? That means that if you sell to open the put, you have the cash in your account that could be used in order to buy the shares of stock. This may not be the best strategy around, but I suppose that it could be better than putting your money in the bank given that interest rates are so low. So the way things work in this case is that you have some money rather than shares of stock that would be tied up each month and you would sell put options against it to generate income.

So in this case having to tie up $14,000, if we earn $538 selling a put option you could think of this as earning 3.84% within a single month on that $14,000. When you look at it this way, that is actually a pretty good use of cash. Of course, it's a high-risk adventure because there is a chance that you would be assigned. In this case, what that means is that you would have to buy the shares of stock. And we are assuming that the price of the shares has dropped so you are going to be taking a loss in some sense. However, it's not like you're being kicked out onto the street. Although you did lose the $14,000, you now own 100 shares of some stock.

People who sell protected puts are going to choose stocks that they wouldn't mind owning at the strike price. So maybe just for an example, you sold a put on IBM at $132 a share. Maybe for some reason, IBM drops below that and the option is exercised so you have to buy the shares. Over time, that probably is not going to be a bad deal. It would be likely that the market price of IBM is probably going to climb back above the $132 price. And another thing to consider is maybe you just want to keep the shares. You could also be selling call options against the shares while you waited for the price to rise.

When it comes to selling put options, the same strategies should be used. So one of those strategies would be that rather than simply waiting for the option to expire and having to buy the shares, a smart options trader would buy the options back before expiration. Second, you would probably want to choose a strike price wisely so that you wouldn't be put in a position of having to buy the shares. But the point of the previous discussion was that in the event that you are assigned and you have the cash in your account to buy the shares, is not exactly a catastrophic situation.

Although protected puts are one way that you can make income, in the grand scheme of things you probably wouldn't want to be doing this. As we will see later on in the book there are better ways to make money while having to put down far less capital. We can even do this selling put options as we will see in chapters seven and eight.

LEAPS

The next topic we are going to consider in this chapter is a specialized type of options contract called a LEAP. To be honest there's actually not really anything that is specialized about these options. This is simply a term used to refer to options that have expiration dates one to two years into the future. The fact that they expire so far into the future does offer some interesting possibilities because they really aren't affected buy time decay the way that options that are closer to expiration are.

One thing that you can do with these is simply to buy them when you're confident that the stock price is going to move in a particular direction. These options have pretty high prices because they expire so far in the future. So, for example, you could buy a call option and then wait for the price of the stock to rise. The advantage of these options that expire so far into the future is that you have a really long time where you could wait for the price of the underlying stock to move in a direction that would make the option significantly profitable for you. The real downside to this strategy is that these are more expensive buy a pretty large margin as compared to options that expire within a month or a week. But if you are able to spend the money to purchase them it would offer a possibility of learning some profit in this way.

There could be another downside, however. One of the things that you have to worry about whether you are trading stocks or selling options is the liquidity of the underlying security. So when you are buying leaps one of the things you want to check is the open interest. Make sure that the open interest is at least 100. If it's above 100 that's even better. Open interest for those who don't recall is the number of contracts that are on the market. It gives you an indication of how many buyers there might be when you need to sell it. So for example going back to the QQQ NASDAQ Exchange traded fund, looking two years out, we find hey $186 call which is $18.52 per share, making the total price of the option $1852. So it's almost 5 times as expensive as the same strike price that expires within a month. The open interest is 406. So this would actually be a good one to invest in if you thought the price of QQQ was going to rise in the future. Of course, the expiration date is so far away you definitely have lots of time to wait for this to happen.

Selling Calls Against LEAPS

So if you recall an option gives you control of 100 shares of stock. It turns out that you can use a call option that is a LEAP for an interesting strategy that is known as the poor man's covered call. Using this method you can actually sell short-term call options against the LEAP. This is possible and it saves you a lot of money. That is as far as having to invest in the stock. So we saw that the option would cost us $1852. But the share price is almost $187 so to buy 100 shares it would cost us $18,700. In other words, we'd have to spend 10 times as much money. So this method is something that you can use in order to sell covered calls without buying the stock.

Summary

So let's review what we have learned in this chapter. What we've covered here are the possibilities that anyone who has a brokerage account can use as a strategy to sell options. The strategies in this chapter require some type of asset to back up the contract. They cover call requires 100 shares of stock that you own in order to sell options against it. This can be used to generate a monthly income. Another way to generate a monthly income is to use cash instead of shares of stock and then earned money by selling put options. Finally, we talked about the poor man's covered call which utilizes LEAPS to sell call options. This is a money saver as far as an investment because investing in LEAPS costs a lot less money than actually buying 100 shares of stock.

Chapter 3: Trading With the Trend

In this chapter, we are going to move on to considering basic options trading. This is probably what most people think about when they are thinking about options. Although the concept involved in this chapter is simple, it is considered a higher risk activity than the strategies outlined in the previous chapter. Of course, most people only trade one or two contracts at a time and so they aren't risking all that much money. But doing this right is actually pretty tricky. What we are talking about in this chapter is simply buying to open an options contract and just buying individual calls or puts. So we are not talking about using any complicated strategies of the kind that we are going to talk about in the later chapters.

Buying Calls

So let's get started by considering the most basic strategy of all, and that is buying a call option because you believe that the price of the stock is going to increase in the near future. Our consideration in this chapter does not involve buying or selling a stock, we are only going to be talking about trading options. Therefore the goal was buying a call option would be to purchase it at the right moment and then hope that the stock will go up so much that we are able to sell the option for a profit. This all sounds simple enough almost like something that you could never miss. Unfortunately, in practice, it's actually a lot more challenging than it sounds on paper.

The first consideration is going to be whether or not you purchase an option that is in the money or out of the money. If this strategy works maybe that is not really an important consideration provided that it's not too far out of the money. The reason that people decide to purchase out of the money options is that they are cheaper as compared to in the money options. It's also a fact that if the stock is moving in the right direction out of the money options will gain at price as well.

So if someone tells you that you can't make profits from out of the money options they are not being completely honest with you. In fact, you can make profits but it's always going to depend on how the stock is moving and the distance between your strike price and the share price.

The best strategy to use when going with out of the money options is to purchase them slightly out of the money by a dollar or two. What this does is it ensures the price of the option is going to be significantly impacted by changes in the stock price. Second, you wouldn't be purchasing a call unless there was a good chance that the share price would be moving up. So if you are close in price to the market price, and there is a reasonable amount of time until expiration, there would be a good chance that the share price would actually rise above your strike price. If that happens it could mean significant profits for you.

Of course, you can always take the risk of putting it a little bit more money upfront and investing in a call option that is already in the money. If the stock price rises, that is only going to solidify your position. You also have a little bit of insurance there. That comes from the fact that if you choose a decent strike price there is a solid chance it will stay in the money and so even if it doesn't gain much value you will be able to sell it and either not lose that much, or still make a profit.

So what are we hoping for with this strategy? The main hope would be that there is a large trend that takes off so that we can write the trend and earn a healthy profit. Since options are so sensitive to the price of the stock if such a trend occurs it's pretty easy to make decent money. The key, of course, is getting in the trend at the right time and knowing when to get out of the position.

Market Awareness

The first thing to keep in mind is what I call market awareness. This involves being aware of everything that could possibly impact the price of the underlying stock. This can mean not only paying attention to the chart of the stock, but you also need to be paying attention to the news and not just financial news. So let's take a recent example by looking at Facebook. In recent months Facebook has been constantly in the news. Some of the news has been good such as a decent earnings report. On the other hand, Facebook has been receiving some pushback from governments around the world. One of the issues that have been raised is privacy concerns. Facebook is also catching a lot of flak over its plan to create a cryptocurrency.

So here is the point. Every time one of these news items comes out, it's a potential for a trend. But there are a couple of problems with this. In many cases, you simply don't know when dramatic news is going to come out. So you have to be paying attention at all times and have your money ready to go. The best-case scenario is purchasing an option for the day before some large event. People are often reacting strongly in the markets when there is a good or bad jobs report or the GDP number is about to come out. So what you would want to do in that case is first of all pay attention to the news and see what the expectations are of all the market watchers that everyone pays attention to. Of course, they are often off the mark but it gives you some kind of idea where things might be heading. If a good jobs report is expected, then you might want to invest in an index fund such as DIA which is for the Dow Jones industrial average. One thing you know is that a good jobs report is going to send the Dow and the S&P 500 up by large amounts. So the key is to be prepared by purchasing your options the day before. But on the other hand you might be wrong with your guess, which could be costly.

You could wait until the news actually comes out. But I have to say from my experience trading this is a difficult proposition. The reason is you would be surprised how quickly the price rises when dramatic news comes out either way. So when one sense is a safer way to approach things but the price might be rising so fast that you find it nearly impossible to actually purchase the options. That you can execute a trade the trend might even be over. But if you're there in the middle of the action you might as well try and then you can ride it out and probably make pretty good profits.

Some people like to sit around and study stock market charts. During the course of everyday trading when there hasn't been any dramatic news announcement or something like that which will massively impact the price of the underlying stock, looking at candlesticks charts along with moving averages can give you a good idea of went to enter or exit trades. However, it's fair to say that there is a little bit of hype surrounding these tools. The fact is they don't always work because they are easily misled or maybe it's the human mind that is misled by short term changes that go against the main trend but is temporary. So you can make the mistake while following candlesticks and moving averages of seeing evidence of the sudden downtrend and then selling your position, only to find out that the downtrend wasn't real and it was only a temporary setback soon followed by a resumption of the main trend. So that is something to be careful about.

Setting Profit Goals

If you were going to trade this way probably the best thing to do is to set a specific level of modest profit to use as a goal. One that I use is $50 per options contract. Some people may be more conservative so you could set a goal of $30 profit. Some people might be more risk-oriented. I would honestly discourage that kind of thinking because sitting there hoping for $100 dollars profit per contract, while it is possible, you may also find yourself in a situation more often than not where you lose money. What might happen is you have to sit around waiting too long to hit that magic number and it never materializes. Options can quickly turn from winners into losers because they magnify the changes in the underlying stock price by 100. So it's very easy to lose money quickly.

In my experience, the $50 price level is pretty good. The only time that this value has hurt me is when I see the $50 profit hit and I failed to sell my positions because I got greedy watching the upward trend and hoped for even more money. So that is something you should avoid it's better to stick to your law, whatever you happen to pick, and then always implemented no matter what the situation is. Remember that there is always another day to trade. You're trading career never depends on a single trade or a single days trading. The bottom line is that it's better to take a small profit her option contract and per trade and then go back and trade some more, then it is to hope for large profits that may never materialize. Also, you can always magnify small profits by trading multiple options at once. So if you trade 10 options and you're only going to accept a $30 profit on the trade, that means in total you could make $300. It doesn't really matter what specific number you pick, but you should pick a value and stick to it. If I have a regret from trading the only regret is that I didn't stick to the rules that I have set for myself.

Day Trading?

For those who are not aware, if you are labeled a patterned day trader, you need to have $25,000 in your account, and you need to open a margin account. So for most individual traders with small accounts, the last thing you want is to be labeled as a day trader. However, since options lose a lot of value from time decay, and many trends are short-lived, you may find yourself in situations where you have to enter a day trade. But if you are doing this make sure that you only do three per five day trading period. That way you will avoid getting the designation and all the problems that might come about with it. In this case, if you buy a lot of several options that have the same strike price and the same expiration date, those are going to count as the same security. That may result in problems if you need to unload them all on the same day. One way to get around this is to purchase call options with slightly different strike prices instead of getting a bunch with all the same strike price. Of course, if you were going to hold your positions overnight and risk the loss from time decay having to do that may not be something to worry about.

Trading Puts

Trading puts using these techniques is going to be basically the same, with the only difference being that you would be looking for downward trends. This is actually a little bit different because people are accustomed to thinking in terms of rising stock prices means profits. So it might be hard to wrap your mind around the idea of profiting from stock market declines. But you should never ignore the possibility of making money with puts. A successful options trader is going to be versatile. So you should be able to move in between calls and puts pretty easily depending on market conditions. So when bad news comes out this is a huge opportunity to make money buying put options and then selling them for more money as the price drops. It doesn't matter if the bad news is political, economic, financial, or are related to a specific company. If the bad news is general in nature then purchase an option for an exchange traded fund that tracks the entire market. Or a great one to use is SPY for the S&P 500. You can use that one for good or bad news of a general nature. So if it was announced that there was a really good jobs report, buying a call option on SPY, is what you would want to do. On the other hand, if there is some news like China announcing retaliatory tariffs, you would probably want to buy a put option instead.

Range Trading

Some people think that they have to wait for a big stock move in order to make profits. But that's simply isn't the case. You can also look for stocks that are engaged in a pattern that is called ranging. This is a situation where the stock is moving up and down within a range but it's not breaking out either up or down. This requires a little bit of patience because you have to watch the stock for a while in order to determine what the range is. The lowest price that is reached is called the support level price. You want to see the price Drop down and touch this level two times. When a stock is ranging it's going to touch that support level price, and then rise up to a peak value that represents what is called the resistance. So obviously the best time to buy a call option would be when the market price goes down to the support level. Then all you do is whole onto the option until the market price rises back up to the resistance level.

If we were trading put options on a ranging stock, we would do the same technique but in the opposite manner. So, in this case, we want to purchase the options when the stock is at the top value. Then you just wait for it to drop back down to the support level price and you can sell your put option for a profit at that time.

Swing Trading

You can basically swing trade using options. The only difference that has to be taken into account is the fact that time decay may inhibit your ability to hold the position long enough in order to profit. So swing trading would involve looking for our price swing. It's going to have to be something that occurs over a day or two at the most. Otherwise, the price might not move high enough in order to fight against the time decay. So if you're doing this with call options you are going to look for the stock hitting the low price that it's probably going to hit all other things being equal. Then you would buy your call option at that time. From here on out you just sit and wait until the price rises back to the resistance level. You want to be disciplined about it and don't start hoping that there is going to be a breakout and price. Just take your profits while you can get them and then you can enter more trades later.

Chapter 4: Earning Money No Matter How the Stock Moves

One of the difficulties went straight up trading using call and put options is that you can always be sure the stock price is going to move but you may not be sure which direction. For example, if we are buying options before hey jobs report, it's virtually impossible to tell ahead of time how the market is going to react unless the jobs report is particularly dramatic. One of the situations that really drives this point home is earnings season. People are always lining up to trade options at earnings season because the underlying stocks typically make huge moves. It's a rare occasion when a company exactly meets the expectations of the analysts.

The problem is before the earnings of the company are reported you don't know which way the stock is going to go. Wouldn't it be nice if you could make profits anyway the stock moved? Well, it turns out that you can. And that's what we are going to investigate in this chapter. The method that is used is to buy a strangle or astraddle. We are going to explain how they work in this chapter.

The Two Strategies: Straddle and Strangle

The primary goal here is to set up a strategy to earn profits when there is a large price movement of a stock. Furthermore, we are looking for strategies that will earn provides if the stock moves either up or down at price.

There are two strategies that you can use to make profits no matter what direction the stock moves. These are called straddle and strangle. With these strategies, we will be purchasing a put and a call at the same time. It will cost more to enter the trade than just buying a call or a put on their own, but as we'll see the probability of having a winning trade is increased.

A straddle has a put and a call with the same strike price and expiration date. A strangle has a put and a call with different strike prices but the same expiration date. Either way, the position is going to have a range over which you lose money, that will be in the middle of two break-even prices. There will be a higher break-even price and a lower break-even price. If the stock ends up in between these two prices, you will lose money but the loss is limited. If the stock moves above the higher break-even price or goes below the lower breakeven price, this is when you will make profits.

When to use these Strategies

You use these strategies when the stock is expected to make a big move, but the direction of the movement is uncertain. The classic example of when to use a strangle or a straddle is when there is an upcoming earnings call. The trader will buy the options a few weeks before the earnings call, or at least one week before the earnings call, in order to take advantage of volatility. Implied volatility can make the prices of options rise, and as an earnings call approaches, especially for a hot stock like Amazon or Netflix, implied volatility is going to increase by a significant amount. By purchasing the options early, the trader ensures that they have bought them at the best possible price. However, since the stock is likely to move by fairly significant amounts, you can still enter a strangle or straddle the day before an earnings call, but it will be more expensive. The movement of the stock the following day after the earnings call will probably more than makeup for it.

Another time to use this type of strategy is when a company is going to have a product announcement or a big news conference. Take Apple as an example. They have events throughout the year where they demonstrate their new devices or their developer's conference. The same kind of phenomenon will take place because investors will be closely watching the new iPhone, for example. If their reaction is excitement, the stock will go up a lot. If the , is a disappointment, the stock will drop. The point here is that before Apple actually shows the new iPhone, nobody knows how the market is going to react, but it's going to react one way or the other. A snazzy new iPhone that will sell well is going to mean a lot of future earnings, so the stock is going to go up in that case.

You can also buy strangles and straddles on index funds. You can do this when major announcements on the economy are expected. The types of announcements to look for where you would apply this strategy include the federal reserve meetings where interest rate changes are coming, jobs reports, or GDP growth announcements. Funds to use in these cases include SPY, QQQ, and DIA, which track the S & P 500, NASDAQ, and Dow Jones Industrial Average, respectively. You could also use other indexes like the Russell 3000.

These Are Risk Limiting Strategies

The purpose of using a strangle or straddle is to adopt a risk-limiting strategy. The risk limitation in these cases works two ways. First, with this setup, you don't care which direction the stock moves. When you buy a call, if the stock moves down you lose money. When you buy a put, if the stock goes up you lose money. With the strategies discussed in this chapter, you will make money either way as long as the move is big enough to overcome the breakeven prices.

The second way that the risk is limited is potential losses are capped. Unlike some of the other strategies, we will discuss in the book, these strategies are not limited reward, however. The reward is lessened as compared to a call or a put alone because you have to account for the one-loss you have. In other words, if the stock price moves high, the put you purchased expires worthless. So you would have to eat that loss, but compared to the gains you are likely to see, it will still put you in a position where you earn profits. Conversely, if the stock price drops, you will have some loss from the call expiring worthless.

Straddle

First, let's talk about straddles. The goal of a straddle is to earn a profit when the stock makes a large price move. The price can move in either direction, up or down. To set up a straddle, you buy a call and a put with the same expiration dates and the same strike prices. This is entered into a single trade.

To set one of these up you pick a strike price that should be reason enough for the market price to cross on dramatic news. Often, after an earnings report, the stock of a company can move up or down by $20, or more. But unless you have insider information, you probably don't know which way the stock is going to head. That is why a straddle is so useful. The way that you set one up is you pick a strike price, and when you buy a call option, and you also buy a put option that has the same strike price and expiration date. What this does is it creates a narrowband that lies about the strike price which defines the range over which your option is not profitable. In order to earn a profit, you need to have a breakout price on the market. That is the price of the stock would break out of this band that determines losses for your position.

The maximum risk is capped to the cost required to buy both options. You would incur the maximum loss if you keep the strategy to the expiration date and both options expire worthlessly. This would happen if the stock price did not move with a magnitude as large as anticipated. Keep in mind that you don't even have to hold a position until the options expire worthlessly. If it is a stock or index fund that is heavily traded, it's usually possible to find a buyer under any circumstances. Why someone would buy this position if it wasn't working out and the expiration date is approaching is anyone's guess, but we don't care about that. If the position is not working out for us we need to get out of it and minimize our losses. Letting the options expire worthlessly would be a silly mistake that will cost you money.

This brings to mind the expiration date. If the earnings call is on Wednesday, August 1, then don't buy a straddle that expires on Friday, August 3. You should leave sometime in the contract so that it will give it some extra value and you have a bit of time to get out of the position if you need to before it really loses value from time decay. So in that situation, you would be better off entering a position that expired Friday August 10 instead, even though the upfront cost will be higher. You are also more likely to find a buyer in that situation if you need to get out of the position because there would be time left for it to turn a profit.

A straddle can make money if the stock price goes up by a significant amount or if the stock price goes down by a significant amount. On the downside, the theoretical maximum profit would be the price of the stock less the cost of the call option and the cost of the put option. What would happen if the stock dropped all the way down to zero? Of course, that is extremely unlikely to happen, but it gives you an idea of the maximum boundary for profits for a declining stock price. This is actually the same as buying a put option, except now we have the added cost of having bought a call option as well. But it has the advantage that we didn't know the direction that the stock would move, and still can make a profit. After earnings calls, price movements can be extreme and so they will more than account for the cost of buying two options. Consider that this past month, Netflix dropped more than $40 a share after hours, the night of the earnings call.

If the stock price rises as a result of the event we are trying to tap into such as an earnings call, in theory, the gains are unlimited. And of course that is also theoretical, a stock might rise $5 a share, $10 a share, or even $40 a share, but it's not going to increase without limit. No matter what it does, however, it is likely that it's going to raise enough to overcome the cost of entering the position and earn profits.

To maximize the chance that you are going to see gains, you should enter positions like this with hot stocks that draw a lot of attention at earnings season. They don't have to all be tech stocks, others to consider could be stocks like Disney, for example.

Calculating breakeven points

Before you enter a straddle you need to know what the breakeven points are. In the graph below, K is the strike price used for both the call and the put purchased to enter the position. We have defined V as the total cost of purchasing both options.

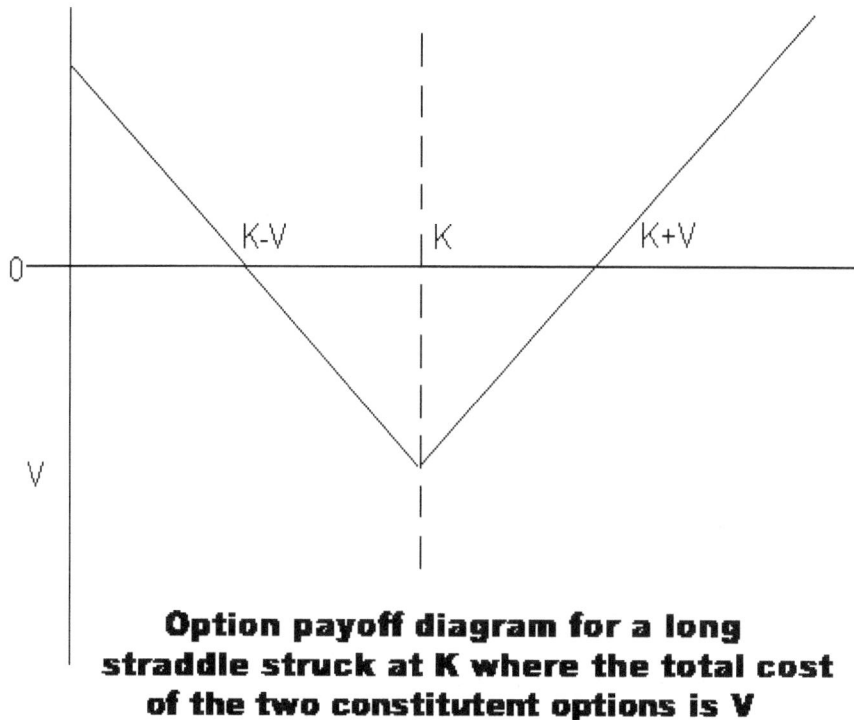

Option payoff diagram for a long straddle struck at K where the total cost of the two constitutent options is V

The break-even points are symmetrical. To the upside, the breakeven price is the strike price + V. On the downside, the breakeven price is the strike price − V. Before entering a straddle, you need to know what these values are, and they have to be selected to have a reasonable chance of success. The more narrow you can make the gap, the more likely it is that you will earn profits.

When you buy the options to enter a straddle, they say that you have entered a long straddle. Remember that earnings calls are likely to cause a major movement in the stock price, but this is not guaranteed. So don't go into these positions thinking that you are guaranteed to earn money.

One of the reasons that you want to enter into a straddle early, and not wait until the night before the earnings call, is that a rise in implied volatility is going to spread out the breakeven prices. A week or two weeks before the earnings call, implied volatility will be lower, and it will be more favorable for you to enter the position. That is because it is going to cost you a lot less to enter the position than it is as the earnings date approaches. If you wait until the night before, the spread of the straddle, that is the price range over which you will have losses, will be wider due to the increase in implied volatility that always happens as it gets closer to the date of the earnings call. So you would need a larger price movement in order to earn a profit, and your profits will be smaller as compared to what they would be entering the position early.

Earnings dates are announced in advance, so if you are planning to use this type of strategy that is something you need to keep track of. Then you should enter your positions early and have the patience to wait for the earnings call to proceed. You can enter the position as soon as the date of the earnings call is known for the company.

How pricing changes for straddles

If the price of the stock hardly moves at all, the straddle price won't change very much either. So we are imagining a situation where the stock price stays about where it was when you entered the position. However, if the stock price rises or falls by a significant amount, then you are going to see a lot of price movement for the straddle. If the price rises, the call option is going to rise in price faster than the put option declines in price. Conversely, when the stock price falls, the put option is going to rise in value faster than the call option is going to lose value.

When to Exit the Position

If you are using this strategy to time to a major event like an earnings call, you should probably sell the position about midday, the day after the earnings call. At the very least you should sell by the end of the day. While it's possible that price movements can still continue the following day, and even a few days after, most of the price movement is going to be captured on the day after the earnings call. Moreover, if there is a big price movement, the shock to the market begins wearing off. So even if a company has a bad earnings call and the stock price drops by a huge amount the day after the earnings call, the following days are likely to see some recovery even if the stock doesn't get anywhere near where it was before the call.

So you shouldn't hold the position hoping to gain more profits as time goes on. More than likely, you are seeing the maximum results that you are going to see the day after and you should be happy with this and take your profits.

In the event you are in a losing position, that is if the stock didn't move enough so that the position was able to at least breakeven, you could consider holding it longer to take the chance that there will be some price movement to minimize your losses. However, remember that time decay is always at work leading to lower options prices with each passing day. And in this type of position, you are long on two options. So both of them are going to be hit with time decay, and if things are not moving in your favor your position might end up worse with each passing day rather than recovering.

The best strategy over the long term for your trading is to get out of positions that didn't work as anticipated as quickly as possible. If the earnings call did not generate the price movement that you were hoping for, then exit the position and accept your losses. Getting out of it quickly will minimize your loss because you won't suffer from any more time decay, and it will free up the capital to move on to your next trade. Losses are a part of the business and you just have to accept them when they occur and pick yourself up and move on to a new trade.

Strangle

The purpose of a strangle is the same as the purpose of a straddle. That is we are entering into a position that will earn money from a large price movement of the underlying stock. The direction of the price movement is not relevant. If the movement is large, the position will earn a profit if the price increases, or if the price decreases. So it is similar in strategy to a straddle but has some differences.

To enter a long strangle, you will buy a call and a put option. They will have the same expiration dates but different strike prices. The total cost of the position is the premiums paid to buy the call and the put option. This is also going to be the maximum loss that you will incur should the position not work out.

The discussion in the previous section with regard to the way of the position and the nuances of implied volatility and when to enter the position are the same here. So you would use a straddle or strangle strategy for the exact same reasons.

Since the options are going to have different strike prices, this will set where the breakeven prices are. This allows you to weight the two breakeven prices. That is, if you think it is more likely that the stock is going to break one direction or another, you can set up the strangle to be more favorable in that direction by choosing your strike prices accordingly.

Many textbook examples show symmetrical choices for strike prices. So if the stock price was currently trading at $100, they might show you an example with a put at $95 and a call at $105. But if you thought it was more likely that the stock would decline in value by a large amount, you could buy a put at $98 and a call at $105.

A graph of a strangle is shown below. In this case, the mid-region between the two options strike prices has the maximum loss, with a linearly increasing curve up to the break-even points on both sides.

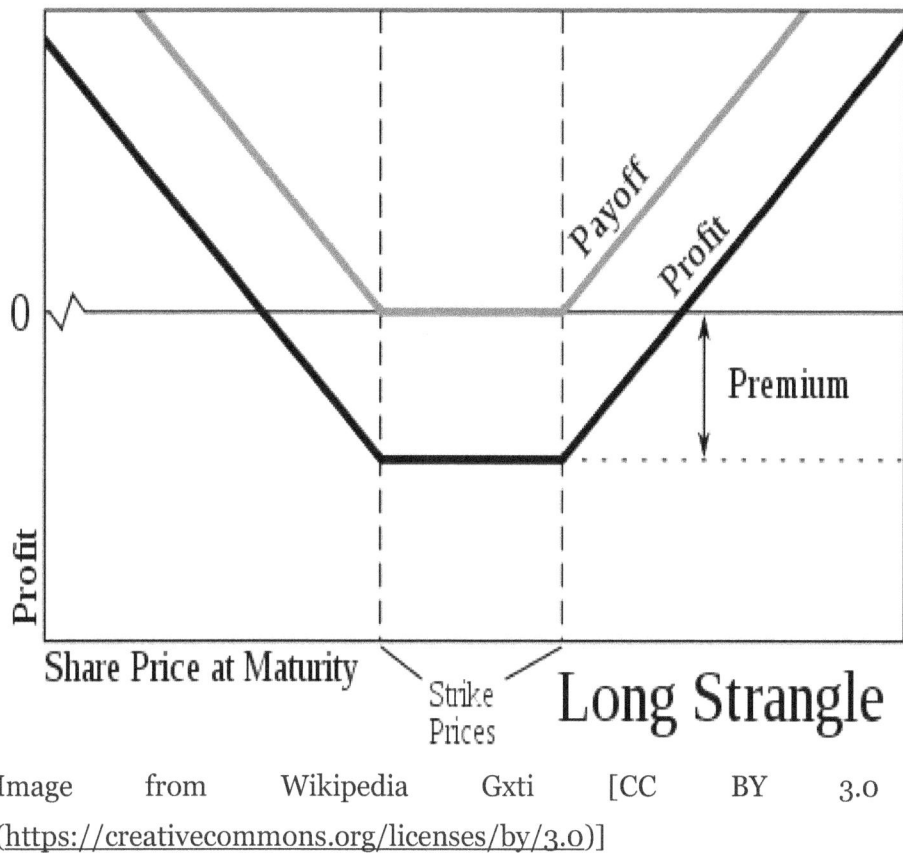

As was the case with a straddle, a strangle is going to be heavily influenced by implied volatility as the date of an event like an earnings call approaches. As soon as you are aware of the date of the upcoming earnings call, you should enter the position so that you can get the best possible prices for the options. Implied volatility is going to cause options prices to increase by large amounts by the time the day of the earnings calls arrives.

Likewise, you should use the same strategies after the earnings call. Earnings calls happen after market close so you should be ready to act the following day. The market reaction after hours is going to give you a good idea of what is going to happen the next day. If the reaction is dramatic, you should be ready to quickly exit your position and take profits. Most of the price action for the day is going to happen within the first half-hour of the trading day. It will then stabilize somewhat but price movements are still possible either way. Sometimes the shock of the earnings call wears off relatively quickly, so you might consider selling to exit your position about two hours after market open.

Summary

When there is a strong trend in the market, buying a call or a put alone is a good strategy. However, there are going to be many times when it is known beforehand that there is going to be a large price movement of major stock, but nobody knows which direction the stock is going to move. This will happen with earnings calls (4 times a year), major product announcements, or a report detailing the findings of an investigation. Or if a company is announcing a major change in management, this can also be a time when a big price movement is coming, but nobody is sure how the market will react. In these situations, a straddle or a strangle is a good strategy to use. Be prepared to enter the position as soon as the date of the event in question is announced, and be prepared to sell to exit the position after the price movement has occurred. Don't hold on to the position after there has been a large price movement and then the stock starts to stabilize, holding on in the hopes of increased profits is usually something that ends up cutting into your returns instead.

Chapter 5: Introduction to Spreads

In this chapter, we are going to return to the case of looking at strategies that can be used when you are anticipating a unidirectional price movement in the stock. So these are strategies that will be employed when you expect the stock to either move up, or to move down. The purpose of the strategies in this chapter is to mitigate possible losses.

The strategies described in this chapter are more advanced because they will involve selling options as well as buying options. This means that you're going to have to have a higher trading level in order to utilize these strategies. Most brokers are going to require level III status in order to trade spreads.

There are two ways that spreads can be used. These are called debit and credit spreads. With a debit spread, you have to pay in order to enter the position. A credit spread is a different type of trade. With a credit spread, you are actually using the strategy in order to earn income. Since the main goals used in the strategies are really quite different we are going to consider them in different chapters. It is a simpler transition in thought process to continue thinking about playing the market to take advantage of either an upward trend in stock price or a drop in stock price in order to make profits. It's also easier to think in terms of buying something to enter the position before considering the possibility of selling something in the marketplace that you don't own. So for that reason, we are going to talk about debit spreads first.

There are two types of debit spreads. The first type is used in anticipation of an increase in the stock price. This is called a call debit spread. It is also known as a Bull debit spread. You can consider the latter term to be slang because most brokers are going to refer to it as a call debit spread. For that reason, we are going to use that terminology.

Likewise, there is a set up they can be used in anticipation of a declining stock price. This is called a put debit spread. Using slang terms, it could also be known as a bear debit spread. But again, when you are entering these positions you aren't going to be doing it on the trading floor you are going to be doing it through your broker. And most brokers use the term put debit spread. So we will also use that term to refer to the strategy in this chapter.

Risk of Assignment

The big difference between the strategy and the ones we've considered so far is that previously we have only considered buying options. These strategies also involve selling options. So there is some risk of assignment when you are selling options. But the risk is mitigated due to the fact that you are not only selling an option you are also buying an option. We will talk about this in more detail when we talk about selling credit spreads because that's more of an issue there than it is here. But let's get a couple of things clear before we move on.

First, let's consider a call option. If you buy a call option, that gives you the option to purchase 100 shares of stock at the strike price. If you sell a call option, you have the obligation to sell 100 shares of stock at the strike price in the event that a buyer of the option decides to exercise it. If that happens we say that you have been assigned. If an options trader is assigned, the broker will alert them to this fact aftermarket clothes on the day that assignment occurred. As we discussed earlier, it's really not very likely although it is possible, to get assigned before the expiration date. It's most likely to happen when an option expires in the money.

For a put option, if you buy it, that gives you the right to sell 100 shares of stock at the strike price. If you sell a put option, you are under obligation to buy 100 shares of stock at the strike price.

The issue with all the strategies going forward is that unlike covered calls and protected puts when you are using the strategies, the options that you're selling are not backed by anything. That's not really true because in the case of a debit spread you have to pay money to enter the position and that is going to define the maximum possible loss. Credit spreads also have to be back to a certain extent. However when we are dealing with calls that we are selling using these strategies we do not have to own any stock in order to execute the strategy. Likewise, any puts that we're selling as part of the strategies are not going to require us to have enough cash on hand to purchase 100 shares of stock. So you really don't have to worry, but we will explain a little bit more when discussing credit spreads.

These are Vertical Spreads

When you read up about options you might hear people talking about vertical or horizontal spreads. In the cases that we are going to talk about in this chapter, they would be considered to be vertical spreads. That is because the two options are going to have the same expiration date but they are going to have different strike prices. The vertical in the spread comes from the different strike prices which are spread higher and lower.

Call Credit Spread

The first strategy that we are going to consider in this chapter is a call credit spread. Remember that if you're reading about this online some people may refer to it like a bull call spread or a bull credit spread. The purpose of this strategy is to follow the same type of strategy that you would use buying a call option on its own. So with this strategy, you would enter the position with the assumption that the stock price is going to rise. So we could say that you are bullish on the stock.

The difference between the two strategies is that this strategy is going to limit your losses. Of course with a regular call option, your losses are limited to the premium paid. What this strategy is going to do is it will cut the amount of lost down further. However, although the theoretical gain from a call option is unlimited, a call credit spread caps potential profit.

For that reason, this type of strategy is called a limited risk and limited rewards strategy. In fact, the potential gain using this strategy is not just limited it's basically fixed. To illustrate this you can see the figure below. This is a call debit spread for QQQ, the NASDAQ Exchange traded fund, with strike prices of $200 and $192. The loss that can occur is fixed for most of the range of possible share prices. However, the gain is also fixed for most of the range of possible share prices. The losses for this strategy occur to the downside. So that is the same as with a call option. Likewise, the gain occurs to the upside.

✕

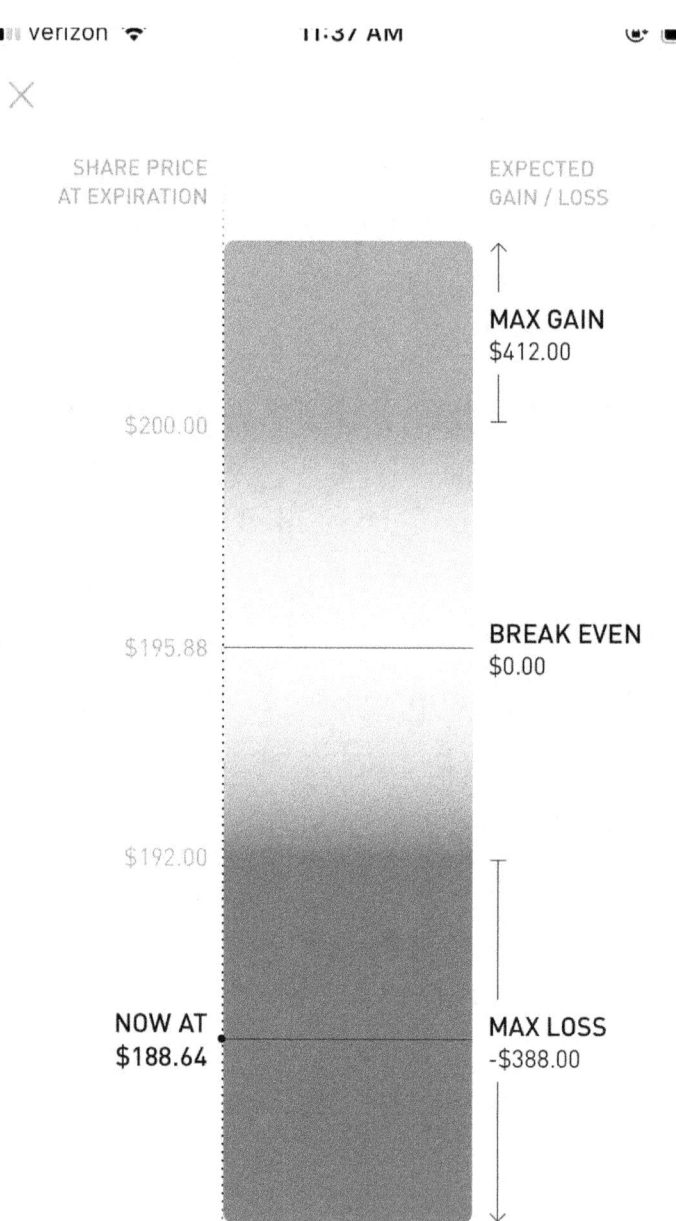

SHARE PRICE
AT EXPIRATION

EXPECTED
GAIN / LOSS

↑

MAX GAIN
$412.00

$200.00

$195.88

BREAK EVEN
$0.00

$192.00

NOW AT
$188.64

MAX LOSS
-$388.00

↓

Although you are trading some possible gain to the upside
you really are losing all that much. First of all, you need to

consider that in the vast majority of situations the stock price is not going to move more than one standard deviation over the kind of time periods that we are talking about for most trades. Most options traders are focused on one week to one-month time frames. Certainly, over one week unless there is a dramatic event of some kind, it's extremely unlikely to see a price movement outside of one standard deviation. That is even true over a month time frame most of the time. So the reality is that although it seems like you're giving up a lot of potential upsides, you really aren't doing so. You are also significantly managing the possible losses that could occur. The example above is for a longer-term trade. So that would mean the cost of buying a call option on alone would be pretty expensive. In fact if we just bought a call option alone, we could be looking at losses of about $780.

Most Professional Traders Don't Buy Calls

When you look at it that way you should be noticing that this trade has a lot of advantages as compared to buying a call option by itself. Sure, there is a bit of a downside in that your profits are limited. But if the probability of getting higher profits is not really that good, that should make it clear to most readers that a debit spread is a better trade. It also benefits from the capped losses, that are going to be smaller in magnitude as compared to buying a call option alone.

The implications of this are clear. Professional traders are going to use this strategy instead of simply buying call options. Amateurs are more likely to buy call options by themselves. And of course, the same logic is going to apply to the case of put options. It is simply a fact that new traders who are naïve are the ones that only by call and put options in isolation. The probability of racking up a profitable streak of winning trades buying call and put options in isolation is low. Many times new traders are going to enter into a position and have a big win buying either a call option or put option in isolation. This will fool them into thinking that is an easy way to make money. But if you try doing this on a day-to-day basis doing multiple trades, what you will find is in most cases it's very hard to make profitable business or to make living trading that way.

So what a strategy like this does, is that although you are trading away some of the potential gains, by limiting the losses it makes it easier to generate a profitable streak of trades over a long time period. So just as a simple example, we could imagine executing the trade shown in the graph over and over again and sometimes it's going to work but other times it won't work. Each time it doesn't work assuming that we get maximum loss, you would lose $388. But as we noted earlier the equivalent call option would have a cost of $780, so each time you had a loss you would be losing nearly $400 more. Solve your losses with the call option in isolation, are significantly magnified in comparison. So that makes it just very difficult to generate a profitable streak as compared to using a debit spread. Remember that if you want to earn living trading, some of your trades are going to be losses and some of your trades are going to win. And what you need to have happened is that by the end of the month the money you earn from wins is going to outpace the money that you lost. It's just common sense business.

Something else to consider is that although a call option in isolation has the potential to earn a lot more money when you do the analysis of a lot of these cases, the stock price would have to rise quite a bit more to earn the same amount of money. Because of the strategy used with the debit spread, we will have some advantages in the choice of our strike prices. So when the two examples that I considered, to make $488 dollars in profit the debit spread would require the share price to rise to $200. The call option and in contrast would require the share price to rise to $208. Of course if the share price goes above that the call option and isolation would earn far more profits. But the probability of that happening small.

But keep in mind that that is not the reason that you enter into a call debit spread. The reason to do so is to mitigate your loss on the downside.

Call Debit Spread Setup

The set up of a call debit spread is actually quite simple. It involves two call options. You are going to buy one call option, and you are going to sell one call option. While you could do this separately since it involves selling a call option, doing it separately would require level 4 trading status if you were not able to sell a covered call. But chances are people using this strategy are going to be people that don't own the stock. And if you are not a level 4 trader, you can't sell naked calls.

Therefore you are going to be entering this position simultaneously buying and selling the call. All brokers allow you to do this in a single order.

With a call debit spread, you buy a call option with a low strike price. That is going to make it more expensive. Then you sell a call option with a higher strike price, and the price of that option is going to be lower since call options with higher strike prices are cheaper. You are hoping to make a profit from the option that you buy in this case. By selling the higher-priced call option, you lower the cost of entering the transaction. Both call options are going to have the same expiration date. The call option that you buy is known as the long call, and the call option that you sell is known as the short call.

This type of position works as a call option in that it will earn a profit if the stock price rises.

Call Debit Spread Risk

The maximum risk that occurs with the call debit spread is going to come from the cost of entering into that position. When you sell an option, you get paid. So you will receive a credit to your account. So to calculate the cost of a call debit spread, you take the cost of the lower strike price option that you buy, and then subtract the credit you receive for selling the higher strike price option.

This value is also your maximum risk on the trade.

Call Debit Spread Profits

Now let's see how we would calculate the maximum gain that we can get buying a call debit spread. This is calculated as follows. The profit that you can earn with a call debit spread is the difference between the strike prices minus the net cost of entering the trade. So let's use a real example so that you can understand how this works.

Consider a call debit spread for the ETF QQQ. We will buy a call option with a strike price of $188. The cost is $3.81 (remember that is a per share quote, so the actual price is $381 for 100 shares). Now we will sell a call option with a strike price of $192. This will give us a credit of $1.68 per share.

The cost of entering the call debit spread would be the cost of the lower strike price option minus the credit received. So this is:

$3.81 - $1.68 = $2.13

That also represents our maximum risk or loss for the trade. Had we bought the $188 call option by itself, the maximum loss would have been $381. So you see that by using a call debit spread instead, we have lowered the maximum possible loss to $213.

However, we've limited the maximum gains as well, decided to cap our possible gain in exchange for limiting the loss. As we said earlier, this is the smart thing to do, because it's not likely that under normal circumstances the share price is going to rise by a massive amount. It takes earth-shattering news for that to happen. Of course, it can and does happen, but most of the time it's not likely. So this is the smarter trade.

Now we calculate the difference in share prices. This is:

$192 - $188 = $4

Then we subtract the cost of entering the trade:

$4 - $2.13 = $1.87

Multiplying by 100 shares, the profit we can earn on this trade is $187.

When Does a Call Debit Spread Earn Profit

The question now is what is the condition under which this trade will earn a profit? The maximum profit will occur if the stock price rises to the strike price of the call option that you sold. If the stock price is at or above the strike price of the short call you get maximum profits. The profits are fixed, so if this happens you should close the position and take your profits. If it is close to expiration you could hold on and hope that it expires in this condition, but there would be a possibility the stock price could drop again and lower your profits.

You will still earn profits if the stock price is lower than the strike price of the short call, but above the break-even price. However, they will be smaller in magnitude.

The breakeven price for this strategy is given by:

The strike price of long call + Net Cost to Buy Debit Spread

In the previous example, the net cost was $2.13, and the long strike price was $188. So the break-even point would be:

Breakeven price = $188 + $2.13 = $190.13

The diagram showing profits and loss with the breakeven price is shown below. Image created by Suicup for Wikipedia. The dashed blue lines show the curves for each option alone, while the red line shows the curve for the call debit spread. Notice that the break-even price for the spread (when the curve crosses the x-axis) is lower than the break-even price for the call option by itself. In our example, the breakeven price for the $188 call is $191.12. So it is a dollar higher than the breakeven price of the call debit spread, showing that it's more likely to earn profits using a debit spread since a smaller movement of the stock is required to breakeven.

Profit from bull spread using call options

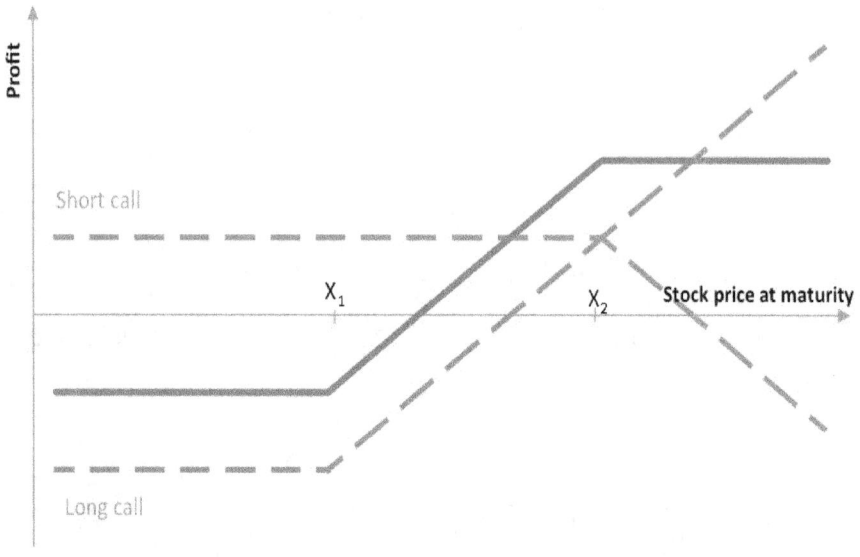

Put Debit Spread

Now we will consider the case of a declining share price. If you think the stock prices going to drop they put debit spread is a risk-limiting strategy that we can use rather than buying a put option in isolation. The benefits of doing so are the same benefits that we saw was a call debit spread. The only difference that is fundamental is that we are anticipating the stock price will decline in this case.

This strategy involves buying a put option and selling a put option simultaneously. So we will have a long put option that is going to have a higher strike price. Then we will have a short put option for the same stock and the same expiration date, with a lower strike price. The net cost of entering this position is going to be the price you pay for the long put option with the higher strike price minus the price received for selling the option with the lower strike price. With put, options remember that the lower the strike price the cheaper the option.

When you enter this position it is going to work similarly to a put option but we are going to have caps on the losses and gains that are possible. This is similar to the previous case of examined. So the maximum profit is going to be fixed rather than having the potential to increase continuously as the stock drops to zero. But we can use the same logic that we applied previously in that under normal circumstances it is definitely unlikely that the stock price is going to drop more than one standard deviation. There is a 68% chance that it will stay within one standard deviation of the current stock price.

In addition, by selling a put option with a lower strike price, we are going to reduce the cost and therefore reduce the possible maximum loss from taking the position. The same effect will also occur with the breakeven price that we saw in the case of the bull spread. That is the breakeven price will be easier to attain using the bear spread approach in comparison to going long on a put option by itself.

Maximum Loss for Put Debit Spread

The maximum total loss that you can incur with a put debit spread is the cost of purchasing the put option with the higher strike price minus the premium you receive for selling the put option with the lower strike price.

Maximum Profit for Put Debit Spread

The maximum profit that you can earn would they put debits spread is going to be given by the difference between the strike prices minus the maximum loss. So let's look at a real example to see how this might work out. This time we will consider they put different spread that expires in one month for Facebook. At the time I am writing this book the share price is $184. So let's look at a slightly in the money put option and choose that for our long put. The $185 put is priced at $5.35. For reference note that the break-even price is $179.65.

Now let's sell the $180 put. Doing so gives us a credit of $3.40.

The total cost of entering the transaction is going to be the price paid for the one $185 put option, minus the credit received for the $180 put option. So that would be $5.35 minus $3.40 for a total cost of one dollar ninety-five. Of course, you have to multiply that by 100 to get the actual cost which would be $195.

Now let's calculate the maximum profit. The difference between the strike prices is five dollars. So to get the maximum profit we subtract the total cost of entering the position from the difference in strike prices. So that would be five dollars minus $1.95. So the maximum profit in this trade is $3.05. Multiplying that by 100 shares, our potential gain is $305.

Break-Even For Put Debit Spread

In the case of a put debit spread, the breakeven price is going to be given by the strike price of the long put(the higher strike price of the two) minus the price paid to enter the position. For our example, our higher-priced strike price for the long put was $185. The total cost answer the position was $1.95. The difference between the two is $183.05. Remember that the breakeven price for the $185 put by itself is $179.65. So not only do we limit losses entering this trade, as compared to the put option by itself, we've also moved the breakeven point closer buy $3.40. So the probability of this trade being profitable is much higher.

Chapter 6: Iron Condors and Iron Butterflies

Often the market is "choppy," meaning that a stock is not trending one way or the other. Of course, stocks don't remain static, so what you will see in these circumstances is that the stock will move up and down by small amounts. This is called ranging. Some traders will attempt to earn money off the small price movements, buying when it hits the low price for the range (called the support) and selling when it his the high price of the range (called the resistance).

However, we don't have to trade that way, we can use a conservative strategy called an iron condor. It makes money when the stock stays within a range of prices and doesn't move very much.

Iron Condor

An iron condor seems complicated, and the reason is it involves four options contracts simultaneously. To trade with iron condors, you have to be a level 3 options trader. An iron condor is a type of spread strategy, but in this case, the idea is to confine the pricing to a range over which the stock stays inside. In a sense, an iron condor is a little bit opposite to a strangle, in that the trader who buys a strangle is hoping that the stock price is going to go outside the range so that they can earn profits. With an iron condor, we are hoping that the price of the stock stays inside the range in order to make profits. However, a strangle is setup only using two options that you buy. An iron condor is a setup using two options you buy and two options you sell.

The upper band of the iron condor

The iron condor is going to have an upper range or band that is made up of two call options. You are going to sell a call with a lower strike price, and then buy a call with a higher strike price.

The lower band of the iron condor

For the lower band of the iron condor, we are going to use puts. So you will sell a put with a high strike price, that is lower than the lower of the two call strike prices. Then you will buy a put with a strike price lower than the first put.

The goal of the Iron Condor

The goal for the iron condor is that the stock will stay within a narrow range of prices. At times you can use an iron condor on any stock, but it might work better on more mature, slow-moving stocks that are likely to be staying within a range of prices most of the time. Compared to other options strategies, the amount of money earned from one contract is going to be relatively modest. You can let the option expire if you are confident that the stock is going to stay trading in the range until the expiration date. If you are concerned that the stock is going to break out of the range before expiration, you can close the position. There is some confusion as to whether you are selling or buying the iron condor, but selling it is a better way to think about it because you are selling two options of higher value and buying two options of lesser value, and you will receive a fixed credit. Therefore to exit the position you would buy the iron condor back. If the stock stayed within the range until that point, time decay would work in your favor and the options will all have declined in value. That means that you will only give up a small amount of money when you buy back the iron condor.

An iron condor is called a limited risk, limited profit strategy. Risk is limited but potential profits are limited as well. The maximum loss of the iron condor depends on whether the stock breaks out to the top or to the bottom. If it breaks out to the top, take the differences between the two strike prices of the calls and subtract the credit received for selling the iron condor. If the stock breaks out to the bottom, then you do the same, but the distance between the strike prices isn't required to match. So you take the differences between the strike prices of the puts and then subtract the credit received.

The profit earned from the iron condor is the net credits received. This is given by:

(credit received for low strike price call – the price paid for higher strike price call) + (credit received for high strike price put – the price paid for low strike price put)

If you want to earn money from iron condors, you might consider slow-moving high priced stocks. Volatile stocks aren't generally good candidates for iron condors, however sometimes even the most volatile of stocks can be in a ranging market.

To sell an iron condor, you need to have collateral on hand. The amount needed is going to be determined by the greater of the two possible losses that can occur, to the upside or to the downside. If the iron condor is symmetrical then the upside and downside are going to have the same possible maximum loss.

As an example, consider an iron condor on Google using strike prices on the calls of $1207.50 and $1212.50, and strike prices on the puts of $1182.50 and $1177.50. The maximum gain is $335, and the maximum loss is the same on both the upside and the downside since the difference in the strike prices is $5 in both directions.

This contract expires in a week, and since the range is actually fairly wide and there are no earnings calls or anything on the horizon, this iron condor is a good trade to consider even though Google is one of the FAANGs and considered a hot stock. If you did 5 contracts you would be required to deposit collateral of $1188. You could earn around $1675 for the trade.

Iron Butterfly

The next strategy that we are going to look at is called an iron butterfly. An iron butterfly is not that different from an iron condor, but we reverse the way that we buy and sell the options contracts. So to set up an iron butterfly you will buy a put with a high strike price, and sell a put with a lower strike price. You will also buy a call with a low strike price and sell a call with a higher strike price.

While you receive a net credit for selling an iron condor, an iron butterfly strategy requires a debit, so you have to pay in order to enter this position. When everything works out it is really going to be the same since you have to have collateral on hand to sell the iron condor, while an iron butterfly is going to result in a net debit and that is the end of it.

In the case of an iron butterfly, the maximum loss is the price paid to enter the position. An iron butterfly differs from an iron condor in another crucial respect. The options that you buy, the put option and the call option, are going to have the same strike price.

To calculate the profit you can earn from an iron butterfly, you take the greatest of the differences between the outside strike prices and the middle strike price. Then you subtract the debit paid to enter the position. As an example, we could set up an iron butterfly by purchasing a put and a call option with a $200 strike price. Then you could sell a call option with a strike price of $205, and sell a put option with a strike price of $195. In each case here, the difference is $5. So we would subtract the net debit required to enter the position. Say that was $3, and so the maximum profit would be $2 per share or $200 for the entire contract.

An iron butterfly has a breakeven point to the upside and to the downside. Take the center strike price used and add the debit paid to get the upside breakeven price, and then take the center strike price and subtract the debit price to get the downside breakeven price.

To make a profit for the iron butterfly, you want the price of the stock to stay within the strike prices on the outside. If the stock price falls below the strike price of the lower put, you are going to be assigned, which will lead to a maximum loss on the downside. The put option with the middle strike price can be used to mitigate the loss. On the other hand, if the stock price rises above the higher call price, you would also be assigned, but that would be mitigated by the call with the middle strike price, limiting you to the maximum possible loss.

So to be profitable, the stock price has to stay in between the range set by the two options that you sold to set up the iron butterfly. If the stock price ends up close to or equal to the middle strike price, you get maximum profits.

Summary

Generally speaking, the iron condor is preferred of the two strategies. The iron condor is considered to be an income-generating strategy. It is a relatively conservative strategy that is used when you believe that the stock is going to be ranging over a narrow band of stock prices. We have seen in the example given with the Google iron condor, that you can set up a rather wide range to use with an iron condor and so you can minimize losses while having a nearly 2:1 or more than 2:1 income to loss ratio. So this can be a good earnings method to generate regular income selling iron condors. If you decided to use this trading strategy, it is recommended that you make it your specialty because it is a rather specialized way to trade, and you should become expert in applying it if you want to be earning a regular income from it. You are probably going to have to spend a great deal of time each week doing research in order to find stocks that will be a good candidate for applying the strategy, and you will have to be prepared in this case to vary the stocks that you use quite a bit week to week.

Many traders use the strategy staring 45 days or 30 days out, and it can be a good way to use it. However, keep in mind that the longer the time frame you use before expiration, the more chance there is going to be for the stock to break out of the range, which would give you the maximum loss. Personally, I think selling iron condors a week before expiration is a better strategy because the short time frame is more likely to be a situation where the stock stays ranging.

Iron butterflies aren't used as much as iron condors, but the principles are basically the same and if you want to go with debits and wait until you sell the position to close it, iron butterflies can be used. Many of the same issues apply in this case. With an iron butterfly, you want to make sure that it is a liquid stock so that you can sell it when you need to.

Chapter 7: Earning Income with Credit Spreads

In this chapter, we are going to change gears and consider using options in order to generate monthly income. This is going to be an entirely different way of looking at options compared to most strategies. So we are going to be looking at options strictly from the position of the seller. For one, it means that time decay and the expiration date are things that work to our advantage rather than being things to worry about. If the strategy is implemented carefully, it is possible to generate a reliable income from week-to-week or monthly. You can use different ways to earn your money depending on how you want to do it.

There is a risk of assignment but it will actually below if you setup your spreads carefully. In addition, we are using spreads to mitigate the risk. As we will see below doing it this way means that we will be able to limit the risk of assignment and if that happens it will all be automatic and our risks and total losses will be limited.

Contrary to public opinion, this is a low-risk strategy if it is done correctly. We are going to explore how to do that in the sections below.

Put Credit Spread Basic Setup

The idea of a put credit spread starts with a similar idea that we saw in the case of a debit spread. That is, we are going to be buying and selling two options simultaneously. They are both going to be the same type (in this case put options) and they are going to have the same expiration date. However, they are going to have different strike prices.

The difference between a credit and a debit spread is that this time we are looking to sell an option that has a higher strike price, and hence more valuable. In the case of a debit spread, the goal is to earn money from the stock price declining. In the case of a put credit spread, we are only hoping that the stock price remains above the higher strike price in our spread. We are not going to earn money from the price movement of the stock, this is an income-generating situation. So we don't really care what the stock does other than hoping that it is going to remain above the higher strike price of the two options. So although some people talk about this as being a "bull" credit spread, or a "bet" that the stock price is going to rise, it really isn't either of those things. If the stock price drops some, but it stays above our strike price, we are still going to make money. In fact, all we really care about is that it stays above the breakeven price.

The risk that is associated with a put credit spread is that the stock will drop by a large amount, that turns out to be big enough so that it drops below the upper strike price in the spread. We will look at the risks involved in detail below.

When NOT to sell a put credit spread

There are certain situations that you want to avoid selling a put credit spread. Under normal conditions, selling put credit spreads is a low-risk activity. However, if you are in a situation where the stock is moving by a large amount, with a lot of selloffs, then it is higher risk.

For that reason, you don't want to sell put credit spreads that are going to be active after an earnings call. As we noted in the chapter on straddles and strangles, an earnings call is one of those times when stock can move by huge amounts. If the stock moves up by a large amount, your put credit spread would be unaffected. If the stock stays about the same or only moves by a small amount, your put credit spread would also be unaffected. But, if the earnings call was negative earnings call that really disappointed investor, the stock price may fall by large amounts – and put your higher strike price put in the money. With that in mind, you want to be conscious of when the earnings call dates are for the companies that you are investing in. And avoid selling put credit spreads during those weeks. Earnings calls are staggered, so when you are on the sidelines with one stock you can be investing in a different stock by selling put credit spreads.

There are other events that can cause your put credit spread to be at risk. A major downturn in the overall market can certainly do so. When the market starts dropping, most stocks are going with it (otherwise the market would not be dropping), and nobody really knows when the stock is going to bottom out. So if this is an ongoing process it might be better to wait on the sidelines or even switch to selling some call credit spreads, which we will discuss below.

However, even in bad markets selling put credit spreads can work. Many very successful traders earned good money continuing to sell put credit spread s(or naked puts as well) during the 2008 financial crisis. The problem with this is you have to be very smart about what you use for your strike prices. Most people will find it easier to switch to selling call credit spreads during these types of situations, including mere "corrections."

Often bad news is hard to predict. At the time of writing, there has been a parade of bad news (as far as the markets are concerned) in the form of what can be described as extrinsic events. That is, these are events that are outside the stock market itself. For example, Trump is involved in his trade war with China. That may or may not be a positive thing, but the markets aren't very happy about it and would like to see a deal worked out. So every time that Trump tweets about raising tariffs, the market goes through a major drop. That could put your positions at risk if you are selling put options. But again, choosing carefully can help avoid too much risk. Also, you can always get out of a position, something that we will be discussing.

The purpose of this trade is to earn income

When you enter into a put credit spread, you get paid for it. The purpose of doing this trade is to earn income. You actually won't see the money until the position is closed. The position can be closed at expiration, or you can close it early by buying it back. So remember that you enter into a position of a put credit spread by SELLING it.

Let's look at some real examples. You can sell a put credit spread for Facebook using the strike prices $170/$155 expiring on 3/20/20, and you would get paid $435. The breakeven price is $165.67. The current share price is $183.45, and so unless something major happens between the time you enter the position and the time you close it out, it is unlikely that you are going to have to worry about the break-even price. Of course, a lot of politicians are babbling about breaking up the tech companies lately, so that could cut into your potential profits in the case of Facebook.

The maximum loss for this put credit spread is $1,065. Your broker will require you to put up $1,065 as collateral for this position. They are not going to withdraw the money from your account. Again, this is because you are selling the spread. But your buying power will be reduced by that amount until you close the position.

That one expires a long time from now, but you can setup put credit spreads that expire in a few days. For example, a put credit spread with strike prices of $182 and $180 that expires in 9 days will pay you $82. The maximum loss is $168. In this case, you would have to put up $168 in collateral.

Now, $82 might not sound like much. But consider the fact that you can enter into as many contracts as you like, and with a highly prized stock like Facebook it's going to be easy to sell them. So you could do ten contracts, and that would give you an income for the week of $820. Not bad for a passive income (well, mostly passive, you should be keeping up with your trades).

An Income Strategy

Of course, you also have to put up collateral for all ten contracts, so that would mean you'd need $1,680 in your account to cover the trades. But this is really an amazing return when you think about it. There is simply no other way to earn money like this. You only have to tie up the $1,680 for about 9 days, and then you'll earn $820 – so you could think of this as a 49% return in just 9 days. Of course, we note for the record that these transactions are not without risk.

As an income strategy, what you would want to do is enter into these types of positions every single week. So that would mean using the collateral you have in your account to repeatedly generate income week after week. Of course, this is not automatic or magic, you are going to have to be careful about the positions you enter and be ready to close them early if they look like they are going bad, to mitigate losses. But many people actually use this strategy to make a living as options traders. Some people use 45 days or one-month time frames, others use about a week as described, and others even sell options on the expiration day. Remember that when you are working with a stock or exchange traded fund that is in high demand, there is always going to be a buyer out there somewhere. We don't have to worry about their motivations for taking the contracts off our hands, our only concern is going to be being able to get out of the trades when we need to. If the stock prices are very favorable then you can just let them expire.

You can increase your weekly or monthly income by putting up more collateral. Consider the difference between doing it this way and selling a protected put. If Facebook is trading at $183 a share, for a protected put, we would have to tie up around $18,300 for a put option that expired in 9 days with a $182 strike price, as collateral. If we sold a $180 strike price put, We would only earn $239 for the trouble.

When you compare that to the put credit spread, where we can sell ten contracts and earn $820, but only tie up $1,680 in collateral, you have to ask why would anyone bother selling a protected put? In my view, there isn't any reason to sell protected puts. In fact, if you have $18k that you can sink in the stock market to use as collateral, you should probably be selling naked put options.

The Risk Reduction Setup of a Put Credit Spread

To sell a put credit spread, you must be a level 3 trader. You are also going to be required to have some capital (aka money) to put up to back the trade. The good news is that the amount of money required is a small fraction of the money that you need to have for a protected put option. You don't need to put up enough cash to actually buy 100 shares of stock. This is because you are protected to a certain extent by the put option that you buy as insurance.

Assignment Risk

To understand the risk reduction of a put credit spread, we will take a look at the risk of assignment. Remember that before expiration, while the risk of assignment is always real, you are more likely to face assignment when the option expires. Second, the break-even price works in your favor to give you a little bit of room in case the stock is dropping.

Let's have another look at Facebook options. We are not concerned with the put option that we buy that has a lower strike price. That one we will exercise on our own if it comes to that because we are playing the role of the buyer in that case. You might be wondering how you are going to exercise the option, especially if you don't have the tens of thousands required to buy Facebook stock, but we will explain that in a minute.

Let's say that we sold a $180 put. The Price is $2.39 for this put currently. So for each put contract that we sell, we receive a credit of $239. This tells us the breakeven price, which is the strike price minus the price paid for the option. In order for it to be worth exercising at all, the share price must drop at least down to the breakeven price. In this case the breakeven price is $180 - $2.39 = $177.61.

So even though the strike price is $180, there are zero risks of assignment unless the share price of Facebook drops all the way down to $177.61. And even then, it's unlikely that you will be assigned. From the buyers perspective, at $177.61, they only break even because they had to pay you $2.39 for the privilege of owning the contract. So while it could happen, an assignment is still unlikely. It's even going to remain unlikely if the price keeps dropping past the break-even point. Someone who has the money to buy the shares on the market is probably not going to be interested in trading 100 shares in order to make $50 or even $100. Of course everyone has different opinions and motivations, so we are not saying it's impossible, we are only saying that it's not likely to happen.

Now let's set up an actual credit spread so that we can get a real idea of what the risks are and what is going to happen.

We are going to set one up that expires in about 2 weeks. To do this we are going to go a bit out of the money – which is the smart way to sell put credit spreads. You are not going to sell an in the money put and risk assignment right away, or certainly risk assignment if the position expires. By moving out of the money, we increase the probability that we are going to earn a profit on the transaction.

The share price is currently $183, so let's pick a strike price of $175. We can sell it for $1.21 per share, or $121 per contract. The probability of earning a profit on this option is 82%. You have to like something that has an 82% chance of profit. It's highly unlikely that in the next two weeks the price of the Facebook stock is going to drop $8 a share. Of course, if the Justice Department announced they were going to break Facebook up, or Mark Zuckerberg was arrested, that would cause that kind of drop. It could happen, but it's not likely to happen.

We want to make a decent amount of money on the transaction, but remember that we can sell many contracts, so we don't have to earn all that much on an individual contract. The more distant the strike price of the put option you are going to buy, the more money you are going to make. However, that also means you have to put up more collateral. Let's try two different schemes.

For the first one, we will pick a price close by. So we will sell the $175 put for $1.21, and we will buy the $172.50 put for $0.87 to create the put credit spread. The net credit for this transaction would be $0.34. So per contract, we're only earning $34. To sell one of these contracts, we need to put up $205 in collateral. To earn some real money, we might sell 20 contracts. That would give us a credit of $680, but we would have to put up $4,309 in collateral.

Now let's see what happens if we go much lower for the option we sell. We are still going to sell the $175 put for $1.21. Now we will buy the $160 put, which is only $0.18. This gives us a nicer net credit at $1.03. We could sell 5 contracts and earn $515. The likelihood of this spread going in the money is very low, remember that the chance of profit is 82%. So this is a good deal.

However, we see that we are required to put up more collateral. The amount needed is going to be $6,974.

Whether one trade is better than the other is going to be a personal decision. The point here is to illustrate that putting a larger spread in the strike prices means that we are going to have to put up more collateral. But note that we only have to sell 5 contracts to earn $500, in the other case to earn around $680 we'd have to sell 20 contracts. In the event we need to close the position, it's going to be easier to close 5 contracts than it is to close 20 contracts.

Closer to current stock price

The closer you get to the current stock price, the more money you can make for less required collateral. The risk of losing trade increases. However, a four-year study showed that one standard deviation put spreads had a 94% success rate, while slightly out of the money put spreads had a 79% success rate. That argues in favor of the one standard deviation out of the money spreads, which is probably the way a more conservative trader would proceed.

But that doesn't tell the whole story. When the profits were added up, the slightly out of the money put spreads earned nearly 3x as much profit. So if you trade closer to the stock price, the higher amount that you can earn means that you are going to make more money over the long run even though you are going to lose more trades.

This time we are going to take a look at a more expensive stock. The advantage of this is the more expensive the stock, the fewer contracts we have to sell in order to make good money. So let's try Google, using GOOGL (they have two stocks). The share price is $1,191. We can sell a credit spread for $1.60 per the contract that expires in one week. Five contracts would give us a credit of $800. The collateral needed is only $1,589.

The strike prices are $1,182 for the upper strike price and $1,177 for the lower strike price. There is some risk here that the stock will fall enough to put at least the upper strike price at risk, but the stock still has to drop $9.

The main point of this exercise, however, is to show that we can earn $800 in one week with only $1,589 in collateral. So the closer you go to the current share price, the less collateral you have to put up, but conversely the higher the risk of the spread. But how real is the risk – under normal circumstances in a bull market or a ranging market it's not going to be that significant? The probability of profit for a GOOGL put option $9 out of the money is 69%. That is a bet that I would take, a 70% chance of profit and you only have to put up $1,500.

But one of the best things about this as compared to the other contracts we looked at is the fact that we can earn $800 a week only trading one, single contract. That means if we need to get out of this contract, it's going to be easier to do.

Breakeven

The breakeven price for a put credit spread is the strike price of the short put (the put option that you sell) minus the net premium received. So to calculate it just take the price of the higher strike price option, and subtract the price of the lower strike price option, and that is the net premium received. Then subtract that from the upper strike price to get the breakeven point

How Assignment works

Let's take a look at the Google example and we will suppose that in fact, the share price drops by a large amount. The example we will consider has an upper strike price of $1,182.50 and a lower strike price of $1,177.50. The breakeven price is $1,180.90. So we don't have to be too concerned unless the stock price drops all the way down from $1,191.58 (today's current price) all the way down to $1,180. If there were a bad earnings call, that would be probable. During the hum-drum market activity, it's extremely unlikely. But let's say that the share price drops to $1,179. What happens in this case?

We would lose $189.81. How did we get that number? If someone were to exercise the higher strike price option, they would sell it to us at the strike price. That means we'd have to buy 100 shares for $1,182.50 per share, or a total of $118,250. WOAH!

So you are probably thinking, where am I going to get $118,250 to buy the shares? Seems like you will have to declare bankruptcy! However, that isn't the case. What happens is your broker buys them for you.

Then they immediately sell them on the open market. For our hypothetical we are setting up, we said that the market price of the shares is $1179, so they can sell them on the open market for a total of $117,900. The loss that we incur is the difference:

Total loss = $118,250 - $117,900 = $350.

Well actually, we need to add in the credit we get for selling the contract. That is about $161. So the actual loss is:

Total loss = $118,250 - $117,900 – Credit = $350 - $161 = $189.

Pretty exciting isn't it? All that money flying around in our account, and we just end up with a $189 loss.

So the assignment isn't something to fret too much about. That is why you are not required to put up the kind of cash that you have to put up in order to do a protected put where you get stuck with the shares. Of course, in that case, you could sell the shares on your own if you wanted to.

Now let's look at what happens in the case of the stock price dropping down even further. If the stock price drops below the strike price of the other put, we can exercise that put to sell shares. We would lose more money in that case, so you might be wondering how the lower strike price put offers protection. The case where it offers protection is when the stock drops by large amounts. Let's say it dropped to $900 a share. If we only had the first put option, we'd be out $28,089. The reason is after being sold the shares at the upper strike price of $1,182.50, we'd be forced to sell them on the market at $900 a share, and in that case, we'd only get back $90,000.

So we'd take a huge loss. This is where the other put protects us. Now, after buying the shares for $118,250, we can exercise the other option that had a strike price of $1,177.50. This brings in $117,750, which is a lot more than $90,000. Now our total loss is:

Total loss = $118,250 - $117,750 - $161 = $339.

So you see how the lower strike price put, which we buy, offers a huge amount of protection in case of a large drop in the stock price.

Pick About 5 Stocks

When implementing a strategy for making an income from put credit spreads, you should stick to about five stocks to use. You don't want to have so many you are interested in that you are not able to keep up with the stocks and the companies. At any given time, you should only be actively trading 2-3 of them. If you want to earn more income, it's better to trade more contracts on one stock than to let things get so big that you are not really able to keep track of all the different stocks. Using this process, you can re-evaluate at the end of the year and change out stocks that are not working for you or if you find something that is more of interest.

Call Credit Spreads

It's also possible to sell call credit spreads. This is a strategy that you would use when you don't expect the stock price to rise high enough to put your spread in the money. A call credit spread has the long and short positions of a call debit spread reversed. That is, you sell a call option with a lower strike price and hence higher option price. Then you buy a call option with a higher strike price. In this situation, the goal is to earn income from selling the option with the lower strike price, and then we mitigate our risk by purchasing the higher-priced option.

In this case, we need to know the break-even point, which his going to be lower strike price plus the net credit received. In order to make maximum profit, the share price is going to have to stay at or below the strike price of the short call.

During a bull market, and often even during bear markets, professional options traders are selling puts. However, a versatile trader will move back and forth between them. If there is a bear market a call credit spread represents a reliable way to earn income. It is really the same strategy as selling a put credit spread but adjusted for different market conditions.

To determine the maximum loss you can incur with a call credit spread, take the differences in the strike prices minus the net credit received for selling the spread. So if you are short a $200 call, long a $210 call, and the net premium received was $5, your maximum loss would be:

($210 - $200 - $5) x 100 = $500

If the stock price rises above the strike price of the lower-priced call option, and the option goes to expiration, you will be assigned. You can also be assigned early although as we've repeatedly said the risk of that happening is low, relatively speaking. So in the case of a call credit spread, you are not going to own the shares, because this is not a covered call. This is going to work something like the put credit spread, the brokerage will step in to make it happen.

So let's say that we have a $200 strike price and the stock price rises to $204, and the option is exercised. So we have to sell 100 shares at $200 per share. The broker will buy the shares on the market at $204, then sell the shares to the buyer at $200 a share on your behalf, and then stick you with the $400 loss.

The higher-priced, long call option that is used as a part of the spread is for our protection if the stock rises by a large amount. Say it rises to $240 a share. The lower strike price option is going to be exercised, which means having to get shares to sell. We get the shares by exercising the $205 option, so we are able to buy 100 shares for $205 each. Then we sell the shares when assigned for the $200 option, with a net loss of $5 per share, for a total of $500. So our loss has been limited to that amount (less the credit received) even though the share price rose to $240 a share.

Buyback Strategy

Remember that you can always implement the buyback strategy discussed earlier in the chapter about selling covered calls. If there is some chance that the stock could make a sudden movement on expiration day, or you find yourself in a position where the closest strike price is in danger of going in the money, you can close your position by buying back the credit spread. Always buy back the credit spread if there is a danger of assignment and it's close to expiration. Don't let it expire.

The Issue of Commissions

In many online treatments regarding options, they are going to note that your expenses include not only losses or premiums paid, but also commissions. These days it's easy to find a zero-commission brokerage. Many beginning options traders can get by using these zero commissions brokerages and do just fine. There is a lot of benefits to using a zero commissions brokerage since you are going to save a lot of money and therefore keep your profits up. One argument against some of these brokers is that they don't always have the kinds of tools that you need. This is true, in some cases. But you have to ask whether or not you really need all of the tools that are available on some of the websites. Also, it's possible to get free access to many stock market analysis tools online.

It's also a simple matter to do all the calculations of breakeven point, maximum profit, and maximum loss just by looking at the formulas which are all simple arithmetic.

In my opinion, you really don't need a computer to be doing all of those calculations for you. But everyone has their preferences, and if you want all that displayed for you on-screen and think that it's going to help you make better trades, you can use platforms like Think or Swim or Tasty Works are probably the two that I would recommend.

If you are looking to earn income from selling put options, one thing to be aware of is that some platforms don't allow you to sell naked puts or calls. As a result, some traders may find them inadequate because they would rather do those types of trades as opposed to selling credit spreads. Certainly selling a naked put is slightly easier than selling a put credit spread, you only have one option to worry about and don't have to try and figure out which spread is the best to use. If you prefer trading naked options then it might be worth paying the commissions, which are going to be small relative to the money made from the trade. But remember that every time you make a trade you have to pay the commission and that can add up over time if you are doing lots of trades.

Chapter 8: Selling Naked Options

In this chapter, we are going to talk about selling naked options. In many ways, selling naked options is easier to deal with than selling spreads. However, in order to sell naked options, you need three things.

- You must be a level 4 options trader.
- You need a margin account (which must have a minimum of $2,000 deposited).
- You will need to have cash on hand to cover your trades.

In many online treatments selling a naked put, options are presented as if you sell the options without any backing whatsoever. However, like selling put credit spreads, you have to have some collateral in place in order to do it. That said, the amount of money you need to put in your account is going to be a lot less than needed to sell a protected put option. Most brokerages use what is called the 25% rule which we will discuss right here.

How much money is needed

The amount of money needed to sell a naked put option is called the margin requirement. It depends on the current share price of the stock, the selling price of the option, and if the option is out of the money. There are two formulas that are considered. The greater value of the three formulas is used.

- (Stock's market price x 25% + Option Selling price – Out of the Money Amount) x 100 shares x # of Contracts
- (stock's market price x 10% + Option selling price) x 100 shares/contract x # of contracts
- Number of contracts x 500

Most of the time it's going to be the 25% formula. So let's see how much we need to sell a Google put option. If we want to make about $1,000 in a week, we can find an option with a per-share price of around $10 that expires in 7 days or so. We can sell a $1,175 put for $12.30. The current share price is $1,191.58. As we said, odds are the broker is going to use the 25% formula, so we calculate 25% of the stocks market price:

0.25 x $1,191.58 = $297.90

The option is out of the money by $1,191.58 - $1,175 = $16.58.

So the formula yields, for one contract:

($297.90 + $12.30 - $16.58) x 100 = $29,322

So selling naked options does take some capital. Of course, to sell a protected put, you would have to have $117,500 in cash in your account, and this is a small fraction of that. But you can see that selling put credit spreads, you could make a similar income without putting up so much cash. Of course, an advantage of this is that you can sell a fairly far out of the money option.

The credit we would receive would be:

$12.30 x 100 = $1,230

Not a bad monthly income. And compared to putting your money in the bank, you would be making a good return. Also, note that with a margin account you can use leverage, so you would only be required to actually put up half of the total amount in cash.

Naked Calls

It is also possible to sell naked calls for income. You can do this at any time, if you feel that the share price is not going to rise above the strike price of the option, and go above the breakeven price. However, remember that you are at risk of assignment in this case. The margin requirement for a naked call is slightly different but similar. Usually, a broker will require 20% of the underlying strike price to sell a naked call.

When selling naked calls, care has to be used. The best time to sell naked calls is during a bear market, and you should sell them one standard deviation above the share price or more. Selling naked calls during a bull market is a risky activity that might not work out well for you.

Normally what traders do, is that during bull market conditions, they are going to sell naked put options. If the market changes course and there is a recession or a bear market, they will switch to selling naked call options. Then when the market recovers again, they return to selling naked put options. Generally speaking, selling naked put options is the more popular activity, and even during stock downturns some traders still sell naked put options, they just go with lower prices, adjusting as the market is adjusting. Of course, this can be a difficult strategy to implement in practice, and there is a high risk of getting yourself into trouble.

There are many short term trends in the market that happen for one reason or another, and the best thing to do in those situations might be to simply wait on the sidelines.

Chapter 9: Trader Mistakes and How to Avoid Them

In this chapter we are going to focus on giving a bit of advice. The purpose of this chapter is going to be to look at the most common mistakes made by novice options traders and how to avoid them. Hopefully most readers who plan actually start trading options will take this advice to heart. Of course, it's one thing to read about these mistakes, and quite another thing to actually be in the midst of trading with real money online, and possibly facing real losses. That said, at least you will have heard about them and maybe when you are in trading difficulty you can look these up and review them as necessary. When you do that, try and relate them to the actual situations that you are involved in when doing your real trades.

Buying calls, without a goal for profits

The first mistake that novice traders tend to make is they start off by trading call options by themselves. This type of trading has a lot of appeal for novice traders because the idea is very simple. All you have to do is bet that the stock is going up and buy a call option and sell it at the right moment to make a profit. As we discussed in the book earlier, this is not a very good strategy, to begin with. Trying to use a crystal ball approach to the markets is simply something that really doesn't work very well. That isn't to say that trying to profit from increases in share price is something that you should avoid altogether, but if you were going to do that what you should do is use one of the more event strategies that mitigate risk while increasing the odds of profit.

That said let's suppose that you are just trading call options. The problem with this is emotion often gets involved. So what happens is a traitor gets lucky one day and they get in on an upward trend of a stock. Then they find themselves getting a little bit giddy and taken over by greed as the potential for income seems to get bigger and bigger. So the trader won't really have an exit plan and they might just sit around waiting to see what happens hoping to make big profits. But what happens most of the time is that suddenly the stock is going to stop rising. The stock market is really a complicated thing over the short term. Over the long-term, the stock market is actually quite predictable. That is why people who were willing to wait 30 years to realize their gains always seem to get their plans to work out. The stock market tends to increase in value over time making that possible.

But over the short-term, the stock market is incredibly chaotic and dominated by all kinds of factors that are interacting simultaneously. These include large institutional traders and hedge funds that have their own motivations which might not lineup with yours. And you also have the mental states of thousands of individual traders interacting simultaneously. You can couple this with the fact that people are often going to panic on the stock market and not make the best decisions.

To avoid getting taken in as a victim of all these factors you have to have a set profit level that you are willing to accept in order to exit a trade. Of course one of the problems is saying you are going to have a set profit level and then actually doing it in practice can end up being trouble. I had this problem myself early on in my trading career. One trade that I remember was I bought a put option after a company had a bad earnings call. It quickly made a lot of money. Within a few minutes, I had made a $75 dollar profit. At the time, I had made a rule for myself that I would sell any option that made a $50 profit. But I got caught up in the heat of the moment and so I didn't sell when I could've taken that good profit. Inexplicably the stock price suddenly started rising. This is one of those things that happens with the psychology of thousands and maybe tens of thousands of investors. When a bad earnings call comes out there is a lot of panics and desire to sell off shares. But at some point, people are going to calm down and the selloff is going to stop. The objective measures that caused the selloff in the first place are probably going to ensure that at least for the near-term future the stock is not going to recover the value that is lost as a result of the earnings call. However, when people's heads cool down, the stock is either going to stabilize or even rise a bit to a new price level. And if you are paying attention that can catch you off guard especially when it comes to options contracts whereby the price movements of the stock are massively magnified. What happened in my case is the price rose enough over couple of hours, that by the time I accepted defeat in the situation, I had turned that $75 gain into a $50 loss. Of course if you set a pricing level like $50 for-profit even then sometimes you're going to end up losing. But that's better than having a loss that I had. Imagine if I had bought 10 contracts.

If it's possible with your trading platform you should put in a limit order to sell the option automatically if a given profit level is realized. That way your emotions are completely removed from the situation.

Not Taking Time Decay into Account

One of the most fundamental properties of options is that they have an expiration date. Novice investors often seem to forget this fact. The reason that many of them forget this fact is actually related to the previous discussion. There is always the hope that if the trade is not going your direction it will recover later. Of course that's always possible. If we were talking about trading stocks for you could actually hold them indefinitely and wait around for the stock price to recover. But in the case of options trading, they have an expression date and lose value every single day. That works against traders that are buying options to open their positions. So it's important to remember how time decay is impacting the value of any contracts that you are holding. You need to factor this into your calculations as far as what's going to happen or not in your trades. If you haven't held options overnight before what happens is soon after market open the next day you will see the price of your options suddenly drop by a large amount. Let's just say that an option is trading at $100 in total value. The way to learn the amount that you are going to lose is to look up the value that is called theta. Theta is given as a negative number and a typical value might be -0.11. That means the price of the option is going to drop by 11% the following day. So if at the close of trading power option is priced at $100, the next morning it will immediately drop to $89. This fact makes recovery of a trait that is not going in our direction a lot more difficult. And if we have to wait two or three days for recovery that can be really painful. You can do the calculation to see how it's going to be dropping every single day yourself.

Not having a stop loss

Day traders and swing traders that are not amateurs but professionals, don't enter into trades without using a stop-loss order. A stop-loss order is a type of limit order that will automatically sell the shares that they have purchased if the stock drops to a certain value. You need to have a similar procedure in place for your options trading. So every time that you enter a trade, set a maximum loss for yourself that you are willing to accept. Then if the option price drops by that amount just sell it and move on. This can be difficult to do because people will always be wondering what is going to happen if they just held on. And in some cases cutting out early you are going to miss opportunities for profits that could have occurred later on. But most of the time, you are going to save yourself from loss and pain. You can't worry about hypothetical situations and worry about would have or should have scenarios. You also can't worry too much about one single trade that you might've missed out on. When trading options you have to worry about the averages of all your trades over a long time period. And since most of the time, when a stock is dropping by large amount you are not going to recover, it is better to cut your losses and move the money into a better trade. When everything is averaged out, that is going to result in better results.

Buying Out of the Money Options

Another mistake made by amateurs is to buy options that are significantly out of the money because they are cheap. When you're training options you should not be looking for bargains. Let's say that a stock is trading at $290 dollars a share. If you were to look at options with a strike price above $300, you could probably find some bargains. In fact, you could probably buy a $303 strike price call for $.10 a share. So you get to own the thing for $10. That might seem like a good deal, but the truth is it's a complete waste of time. Over the lifetime of most options the price is simply not going to move by that amount before the option expires. And so what if you gain 10%. That only means that you earn a dollar. The only time that you should consider investing in options that are far out of the money is with leaps that expire in a year or two. So in this case with the stock trading at $290 a share it would be possible for it to reach $303 in a year or two from now. So that might make sense although they're probably better ways for you to be trading options, it certainly doesn't make sense if you're looking at an option expires in a month or less.

Not trading liquid options

The next mistake to consider is whether or not an option is liquid. We talked about that a little bit earlier in the book. Liquidity for any financial asset means that the financial asset is readily converted into cash. In the case of options trading what it means is you will quickly find a buyer when you put the option up for sale. Options trading can move very fast since they're so sensitive to small changes in the stock price. So if you are trading and option and the trade goes wrong you need to get out of it as quickly as possible. If it takes a long time to find a buyer for your option you may end up holding it until you take huge losses. This is true especially if you're trading multiple contracts at once. If you had 10 contracts on SPY or Facebook or Apple, it would be very easy to sell them off in a matter of seconds. That's because the volume of trading for these stocks is very high. But if you had 10 contracts or even one contract on a stock that very few people are interested in, it might take you a whole day to find someone to buy the option of you. You might even be in a situation where the market maker buys it from you but of course you won't know whether that's the case. But the point is if you are trading you certainly don't want to get a situation where it's an illiquid option. If that happens you might even be stuck with it. Now if we are talking about put credit spreads or naked puts, this is less of an issue but you are still better off sticking to options where is not too hard to find a buyer or seller. Remember the advice we gave her earlier which was that you should stick to options that have an open interest of at least 100. If you check some of the high-volume stocks you're going to find that the open interest is well above that.

Failing to keep up with news

Another mistake made by novice traders his they just enter a trade and then wait to see what happens. You need to be keeping track of your trades very closely and one of the things you need to watch out for is news that suddenly breaks. If the news is bad you need to cut your losses and get out of the trade,that is unless you were investing input options. But you also need to be careful about this as well. You don't want to make the mistake of getting out of an options contract prematurely. So if you see a news item that has negative implications for option that you may be invested in, you want to see if that news item is getting repeated across all of financial networks. If it's not a widespread news item that might indicate that investors don't think it's that important. But if you start seeing it flashing all over the place, that is a good time to consider getting out of the trade. This also relates to the basic point that you need to factor in future events that may impact the price of your option. So mistake that you could make would be selling a put credit spread right before an earnings call. If the earnings call turned out to be a bad one, that could quickly wipe out your put credit spread. So you need to have some environmental awareness and using that example if a company you were interested in selling put credit spreads on has an upcoming's earnings call, wait until after the earnings call and at least one day of stock price movement before you start selling put credit spreads on that company.

Ignoring Index Funds

Novice traders often don't trade index funds and this can be a missed opportunity. Several index funds are good for using straddles and strangles and even for using iron condors. Also, keep in mind that when there is great or bad news index funds offer an opportunity to jump on a rising or falling trend. So any time there is some big news that impacts the entire market consider looking at trend trading with index funds or if you're uncertain try a straddle or strangle strategy.

Taking Positions that are too large

Is it better to trade 10 options contracts that are the same or enter multiple contracts on different stocks? The latter is actually a better strategy. You don't want to be in a large contract, that is trading large lots if you want to call it that. When a thing doesn't work out, that is going to magnify your losses. Try trading three different stocks with multiple contracts if you are hoping to make a certain level of income within a given time period rather than rolling the dice with 10 or 20 contracts for one single option.

Conclusion

Thank you for taking the time to read this book. I hope that you have found it very informative and educational.

Trading options can be a very exciting thing to do. When you have won on your trades, you can become ecstatic. Of course the losses bite, but traders are an optimistic bunch, always hoping for the next opportunity to earn big profits that might be right around the corner.

If you trade without following a strategy, you are not likely to see enough profits to make trading worth doing. Traders that trade without a strategy are going to be wandering around aimlessly, and have a few wins here and there and lots of losses, unsure of what their goals are and where they are going in terms of their end goals.

That is why it's important to develop a specific style of trading focused on trading strategies that work. A long time ago, professional options traders, including those trading very large amounts of money, figured out the many ways that you can structure options trades to meet different goals while mitigating total risks. If applied correctly, these different methods can result in more consistent profits.

The first step is to set a specific goal that you have for your trading. You need to decide if you are going to speculate for short term profits or if you want to set up a system that can generate reliable income. To be completely blunt, it is the rare trader that could do both simultaneously. Some traders do both and manage to be successful, but the vast majority of traders are going to have to stick to one method or the other. So your first step as a budding options trader is to decide which method appeals to you more.

Once you settle on a method, then you should learn the strategies that are best suited for that method. Then you should set an end goal in mind, with stepping stones along the way as well. Don't just dive in saying you plan to have a million dollars at the end of the year. First of all, you should start off by setting a realistic goal. So instead you might say that you want to have a million dollars within three years. Then you need to create milestones along the way that are going to be realistic and attainable, with each milestone helping you get closer to the ultimate goal.

Once you have your plan mapped out, you need to learn the different strategies for your style inside and out. If you are going to be a speculator, betting on the directional moves of stocks, then you will need to learn how to trade calls and puts, how to trade strangles and straddles, and how to trade debit spreads. This will include knowing the break-even and maximum loss for each type of trade, along with knowing the profit you can make with each trade. You should also protect yourself by having acceptable profit levels, and then exiting your positions when you get those profits. You should also have a maximum loss that you are willing to accept in any trade and then get out of the trade if you reach that point, unfortunate as it may be.

Others may find speculation too risky. Earning income from options is a relatively low-risk activity. You are kind of like the dividend investor of the options world. Of course, compared to investing in dividend stocks selling options for income is high-risk activity, but at the same time it requires a tiny fraction of the money. As we saw with many of the examples, with a few thousand dollars you can make $52,000 a year. The thing is, you probably only have to put in money now and then and can continually reuse your collateral to generate income off of relatively small amounts of money. If you put in $3,500 or so, you can even make a six-figure income. Compare that do dividend stocks, where you would probably have to invest a million dollars to earn just $40,000 a year. Yes, it's a much safer way to earn money from the stock market in the sense of chances of losing money. However look at the massive amount of capital that you would have to come up with in order to earn a small amount of income! Options are a much better way to earn money than investing in dividend stocks if you look at it from the perspective of how much money you are required to invest in the first place. Many people, in fact most people, are not going to be able to come up with a million dollars to put in the stock market all at once. But lots of us can come up with $3,500 to invest in order to generate regular income, and we'll make more than twice as much money.

For those that want to open margin accounts, selling naked options is a time tested strategy for earning income. It will require you to be careful, disciplined, and savvy about your trades. It is also going to require you to have good judgment about when you need to buy back an option to get out of a trade. Before trying to sell naked options, you should get some experience with other types of trading so that you have a solid handle on the process. Selling credit spreads is the best preparation for selling naked options. If possible, you should sign up with a broker that has a simulated or demo trading platform. That is another way that you can practice different trading strategies to gain more experience without having to put capital at risk. Some people criticize the practice of using demo accounts because it takes the emotion that is normally associated with trading out of the equation. That is a valid argument, but it's still better to spend some time trading with a demo account to experience how things work even if the emotion is not involved. Studies show that traders that practice with demo accounts come out ahead of traders that just start trading with no experience. But the good thing about options trading is that you can start small to get experience. Therefore, you can just trade one contract at a time, risking maybe a couple of hundred bucks, before you start moving on to big trades.

If a given trading style isn't working out for you, then you can always switch. But you should give it six months to a year before you decide to try something else. Just on an odds perspective, it's more likely that people are going to have more success and be profitable if they are following a selling strategy. No matter which strategy that you decide to follow, you need to become as expert as possible with all the available strategies so that you know exactly what you are doing. So this book should function as an introductory education to the world of options strategies. Please be sure to continue your education elsewhere before trading.

No matter which strategy you decide to adopt, be sure that you learn all the ways to mitigate risk. Remember that if a trade is not going well for you, holding it until expiration is a really bad mistake. That is only going to ensure that you come out of the trade with maximum losses. Any time that you are uncomfortable with a trade you should just get out of the trade. It is better to minimize losses and preserve as much capital as possible so that you can get into new, and possibly better trades.

Thank you again for reading this book, and I hope that you have found it educational and useful. If you enjoyed the book please leave a review for the book on Amazon.

Disclaimer

Please note that *Stock Option Trading Strategies*, Jim Livermore, and anyone related to creating this book are not to be held liable for any results that the reader may gain from trading using these strategies. This book is designed for educational purposes only and should be viewed as such by the reader. Any action the reader takes on the information in this book is solely the responsibility and liability of the reader themselves, no one else.

My FREE Gift for You

If you buy my other title, *"Stock Option Trading"* I will give you the 2 *"Stock Option Trading"* Audiobooks 100% FREE! Stock Option Trading is an excellent title that teaches you all about this trading sector. In that book, we are going to hold you by the hand and explain the many different ways that you can invest and trade in the stock markets and make the kind of money that you need in order to profit from the stock market. We'll talk about the topics of investing and trading in the stock market. You will learn about long term investing and the philosophy of Warren Buffett.

What Should I Read Next?

Swing Trading for Beginners: The 2019/20 Valuable Swing Trading Guide for Learning How to Improve Your Trading Results and Your Finances with the Best Low-Risk Approaches

Swing Trading Option: The Ultimate Trading Guide to Discover Safe and Profitable Trading Strategies for Generating Fast and Secure Profits and Rapid Growth for Your Finances

Stocks Option Trading: Learn and Understand How Everything Works and What Pitfalls you MUST Avoid as a Beginner. Learn How Top Investors Lower Their Cost Basis Using Stock Options

Options Trading: The Best Beginner's Guide with All the Essential Information an Investor Needs on How the Options Market Works and How to Start Trading Options in 2019/2020.

Forex trading strategy: How to Invest with the Most Profitable and Simple Strategies to Make Money Trading Stocks, Options, Forex, Etfs in 2019 / 2020 Working Just 30 Minutes per Day.

www.ingramcontent.com/pod-product-compliance
Lightning Source LLC
Chambersburg PA
CBHW070342220526
45467CB00001B/218